# ON THE TRAIL OF BUDDHISM IN ASIA

*Reflections on Tradition and Practice*

# ON THE TRAIL OF BUDDHISM IN ASIA

## *Reflections on Tradition and Practice*

*Edited by*

Suchandana Chatterjee

and

Susmita Bhattacharya

MAULANA ABUL KALAM AZAD INSTITUTE OF ASIAN STUDIES
KOLKATA

PENTAGON PRESS

*On the Trail of Buddhism in Asia: Reflections on Tradition and Practice*
*Suchandana Chatterjee and Susmita Bhattacharya (Editors)*

First Published in 2016



ISBN 978-81-8274-830-9



*Published by*

PENTAGON PRESS
206, Peacock Lane, Shahpur Jat
New Delhi-110049
Phones: 011-64706243, 26491568
Telefax: 011-26490600
email: rajan@pentagonpress.in
website: www.pentagonpress.in

*Branch Office*
Flat No.213, Athena-2,
Clover Acropolis,
Viman Nagar,
Pune-411014

Printed at Avantika Printers Private Limited.

# CONTENTS

**COMMENTARIES**

# Preface

This monograph is a collection of papers by experts in the field of Buddhist Studies. The volume is largely the product of a panel discussion *Buddhist Studies in India* organized by Maulana Abul Kalam Azad Institute of Asian Studies (MAKAIAS) on 17 June 2013 to mark the beginning of the institutional project *Trailing Buddhism in Asia*. The study aims to integrate ideas and commentaries about a Buddhist presence in the Himalayan space and the maritime belt of South East Asia. It reflects scholarly attention that is not just limited to the philosophical content of Buddhism but also relates to the Buddhist world view, the Buddhist way of life and the monastic landscape. The authors further seek to examine the relevance of Buddhism in the era of globalisation reflecting concerns about habitat, environment and heritage. Buddhist Studies represents an amalgam of discourses about a trans-national Buddhist space and inter-Asian cultural connectivity.

The above mentioned ideas emerged in the panellists' discussions about the revival of interest in Buddhist tradition in Asia. Some of that interest has percolated into the realm of Buddhist Studies in India, undertaken by specialised institutes and universities: for example, Nava Nalanda Mahavihara; Centre for Buddhist Studies (Leh); K.J. Somaiya Centre for Buddhist Studies; Department of Buddhist Studies, University of Jammu; School of Buddhist Studies and Civilisation, Gautam Buddha University; Department of Buddhist

Studies, Delhi University and Department of Pali, University of Calcutta. However, Buddhism as a living tradition in Northeast India seems to be left out in this institutionalised range of Buddhist Studies.

The regional interpenetrations and diverse traditions of Buddhism in Asia have been the focus of MAKAIAS-initiated annual symposiums since 2010. The positive feedback to those initiatives encouraged the Institute to expand and extend its research thrust by way of initiating in 2013 the project *Trailing Buddhism in Asia*. The objective of this institutional project is to interact and collaborate with specialised institutions and experts in the field of Buddhist Studies within India and many other regions of Asia. Such interaction, it is hoped, will help to extend the project to newer domains of research. This book is the first in the series that the Institute aims to publish in the course of examining Buddhist cultural links across various regions of Asia.

**Editors**

# CONTRIBUTORS

**Dr. Anand Singh**, School of Buddhist Studies and Civilization, Gautam Buddha University, Greater Noida, Uttar Pradesh. E-mail: anandluims@rediffmail.com

**Dr. Maya Joshi**, Associate Professor in English, Lady Shri Ram College for Women, University of Delhi. E-mail: joshi.maya@gmail.com

**Dr. Sreeradha Datta**, Director, Maulana Abul Kalam Azad Institute of Asian Studies, Kolkata. E-mail: sreeradha@yahoo.com

**Prof. Bela Bhattacharya,** Former Head, Department of Pali, University of Calcutta. E-mail: bhattacharya_bela@yahoo.co.in

**Prof. Lalit Shyam**, Retired Principal, Gorgaon Government College, Shibsagar Dist., Founder Principal, Titabar College and Mahabodhi Pali Vidyalaya and Research Institute, Titabar, Jorhat, Chief Advisor and Former President, All Assam Buddhist Association, Assam. E-mail: shyam.lalit@yahoo.in

**Prof. Madhumita Chattopadhyay,** Department of Philosophy, Jadavpur University. E-mail: madhumita@hotmail.com

**Prof. Mamata Desai**, Retired Head, Department of Ecology, Physical and Human Resources, Kolkata. Formerly with National Atlas and Thematic Mapping Organization, Government of India. Currently

Research Supervisor, Jadavpur University and Netaji Subhas Open University. E-mail: mamata_desai@yahoo.com

**Prof. Ram Nandan Singh,** Professor and Head, Department of Buddhist Studies, University of Jammu. E-mail: rnsingh_@yahoo.co.in

**Prof. Ravindra Panth,** Director/Vice Chancellor, Nava Nalanda Mahavihara, Nalanda, Bihar. E-mail: panthr2001@yahoo.com, nnmdirector@sify.com

**Prof. Sristidhar Dutta**, Former Dean, Faculty of Social Sciences and Former Head, Department of History, Rajiv Gandhi University, Itanagar, Arunachal Pradesh. E-mail: sristidhardutta23@gmail.com

**Prof. Swapna Bhattacharya (Chakraborti),** South and South East Asian Studies, University of Calcutta. E-mail: swapna.caluni@gmail.com

# INTRODUCTION

Indian cultural heritage, philosophy and history are amongst the world's great treasures. Through different historical periods, Indian civilisational influences have impacted the life and culture of Asian countries in various ways. Amongst the many forms of cultural and philosophical heritage that have spread beyond India, Buddhism is undoubtedly one of the most influential and significant.

## Brief History and Spread of Buddhism

Buddhism was founded in India in the 6$^{th}$ century BC. The profound wisdom attained by Siddhartha Gautama, believed by his followers to be a way to end all forms of suffering and live a harmonious, peaceful life, in later years came to be known as Buddhism. Over time, this philosophy and religion reached all corners of the world.

At first, Buddhism spread through the disciples of the Buddha, who travelled widely, preaching and spreading the knowledge they had acquired from him. In the 3$^{rd}$ century BC King Asoka, himself a believer, felt the need for the profound teaching of the Buddha to reach a greater population. Under his patronage the expansion of Buddhism received a further impetus, spreading to the far reaches of Asia. He persistently encouraged Indian missionaries and the disciples of the Buddha to visit other regions to spread the teachings of the Buddha. Even his own son, Mahendra, became a monk, while his daughter, Sangahamitra, became a nun. They went to present-day Sri Lanka as Buddhist missionaries, to spread the message of peace and the teachings of the Buddha. Through such efforts the teachings of the Buddha very soon reached the northwest of India, present-day Pakistan and Afghanistan, and even further afield. In course of time, this region developed some major cultural centres of Buddhism.

In the subsequent centuries, trade routes that developed from this region led to the further dissemination of Buddhism through the journeys undertaken by merchants. Buddhism thus spread from the Kushana kingdom to Khotan, a city in Eastern Turkestan, which also developed as an important centre of Central Asian Buddhism. During the reign of the Kushana ruler Kanishka, Gandhara, a distinctive Greco-Buddhist art form which was a fusion of Asian and Hellenistic art styles, developed in prominence. Buddhist Gandhâran art spread to Afghanistan and to southern Central Asia and Xinjiang, and created several schools across this vast territory. The opening of the Silk Route in the 2$^{nd}$ century BC, led to missionaries and pilgrims travelling between China, Central Asia and India. With the growing interest in Buddhism, the demand for the translation of Buddhist texts also grew. There is evidence of Bactrian and Sogdian translators travelling from Kushana dominions to Eastern Turkestan. One of the renowned translators from Central Asia was Anshigao, who came to China in the middle of the 2$^{nd}$ century. With the increase in the number of Chinese translations of Buddhist texts, Buddhism became more widely known and a Chinese monastic order was formed.

Buddhist monks also visited Thaton, a trading centre in southern Burma (now Myanmar), to spread the Buddha's teachings. With the flow of trade between India and Burma through Thaton, greater interaction led to the further popularity of Buddhism in the region. Despite periodic political changes in that area, the influence of Buddhism did not wane; instead it continued to receive greater acceptance with increasingly large segments of the population. Over time, Buddhism continued to spread, as Japan and Korea also came under the influence of the teachings of the Buddha. Thus, Buddhist texts were translated into several other Asian languages as well.

The expansion of Buddhism throughout most of Asia was characteristically peaceful, occurring over different periods. Interestingly, wherever Buddhism reached, it also adopted from and adapted to local practices and beliefs, giving rise to several strands of Buddhism. As a consequence, the outer manifestation of Buddhist practice, its rituals, became very divergent and varied. However, the inner truths and the fundamental teachings of the Buddha remained unchanged.

Although Buddhism grew into a distinct religious tradition, apart from its religious appeal, many have also adopted the rich philosophical and cultural aspects of Buddhism. Accordingly, its reach was far wider than just its religious aspect. Often, even without directly converting and becoming Buddhists, believers accepted the philosophical and practical aspects of Buddhism and incorporated them into their religious and social practice. As a result, there are people who identify themselves with the living traditions of Buddhism even if they do not identify themselves as Buddhist.

## Intellectual Initiative

At Maulana Abul Kalam Azad of Asian Studies (MAKAIAS) an attempt is being made to understand the historical, social, and cultural milieus from which Buddhism emerged, and its influence upon various religious cultural mores and social conditions that have been touched by it. The impact of the spread of Buddhism and its philosophy was felt on architecture, art, music, literature and food, giving rise to visual materials and documentations that have not only provided different perspectives but also new research on Buddhist phenomena. It is certain that many famous centres of learning that developed in ancient times would not have been feasible without the active participation of teaching monks. The ancient Indian universities of Nalanda and Taxila played a prominent role in the dissemination of Buddhism as a cultural tradition.

For the past two decades, MAKAIAS has been researching on several issues within Asia, and examining the various common strands that exist in the different socio-political and cultural milieus of Asia. It was during a brain-storming session at the 10th Bangladesh-China-India-Myanmar (BCIM) Forum co-hosted by MAKAIAS at Kolkata in 2012, that for the first time we flagged the possibility of viewing Asia through the prism of Buddhism and its manifold manifestations both in the past as well as in the contemporary world.

We felt that, clearly, the teaching and ideas of Buddhism interconnected several regions of Asia, impacting upon political, infrastructural, economic and cultural aspects. While Buddhism has gained strength in some countries in Asia, though elsewhere its influence has weakened due to a number of reasons, Buddhism still remains a significant common cultural factor in the larger part, if not the whole, of Asia. However, despite there being many aspects in common across Asia, there have been no earlier attempts to examine how Buddhism as a religion and a concept evolved and where it now stood, not only as a religion but also as a way of life that continued to influence even those who were not strictly within the Buddhism fold.

The overwhelming response to the initial idea of examining how values and traditions arising out of Buddhism continue to connect the four BCIM countries resulted in the project soon being launched at our Institute.

In the past decade there has been a noticeable resurgence of Buddhism not only in India but elsewhere, and it was apparent that all neighbours were keen to engage with one another through this platform and its activities. The resurgence in the amount of people who have started looking afresh at Buddhism in the last couple of years is suggestive of the importance of such a project.

The Buddhist world view, the Buddhist way of life, the monastic landscape, are interesting aspects of an interactive space that was moulded not merely by philosophical doctrines of Buddhism but by real life experiences of reformist intellectuals and pilgrims, most of whom had, through institutional patronage, crossed difficult geographical barriers like the high mountains and mountain passes of the Altai and Tien Shan region, and desert areas like Cathay. The Asiatic Buddhist space comes to life in the legends and myths, physical connectivity and networking of the Buddhist arena (immortalised through the Silk Route discourse). This volume brings together several essays dealing with various aspects of this heritage, emerging from a seminar in which these subjects were discussed.

A significant contribution, not included in this volume, was offered by Prof Tansen Sen. He focused on the early 20$^{th}$ century Chinese intellectuals led by Liang Qichao who began writing about Buddhist interactions between ancient India and China. Living during the colonial period, their scholarship formed a part of the discourse on Pan-Asianism taking place in Japan, China, and India. Rather than explaining the complexities of multi-ethnic networks, which contributed to the spread of Buddhism, these scholars placed the issue within a statist framework. This discourse became more widespread after the emergence of post-colonial nation-states in the late 1940s. After the India-China conflict of 1962, some scholars in China and India started producing uncritical and propagandist works on Buddhist exchanges to compensate for the political problems between the two countries. The historiography of the Buddhist interactions between the South Asian subcontinent and ancient China by scholars based in India and China was also discussed. Reference was made to the wider political context which influenced the writings of these scholars and led to the distortion of the historical processes through which Buddhism spread across Asia.

A brief overview of the essays in this volume will show the wide range of subjects and perspectives covered in these pages.

Ram Nandan Singh, in *Buddhist Studies in India: A Vital Link for Peace and Prosperity in the Asian Countries*, highlights Buddhism's compatibility with the modern age, and asserts that it has all the qualities and characteristics for achieving and sustaining peace and prosperity in the Asian countries in particular and the world in general. It answers Albert Einstein's description of the religion of the future as a cosmic religion, transcending a personal God, avoiding dogmas and theology, covering both the natural and spiritual. Moreover, the principles and doctrines of Buddhism are congruent with paradigms of modern social mores and dynamics, political thoughts and ideals, philosophical approaches in terms of both the epistemological and the ontological, economic perceptions based on the Middle Path of Buddhism and the ecumenical notions as well as syncretism of Mahayana Buddhism in the framework of Buddhayana. All these principles and doctrines of Buddhism lead towards peace and prosperity in the modern context.

Swapna Bhattacharya (Chakraborti), in *Regional Representation of Myanmar Buddhism in India* offers a reappraisal of the nomenclature 'India-Myanmar Cultural Continuum' and ponders over the following issues: (a) ideas related to the resurgence of *Buddhasasana* in India in which Myanmar monks (*Sayadaw*) have been engaged; and (b) Buddhism practised by the Khamti community of Arunachal Pradesh (Namsai-Tengapani area), to show how the ethnic model of Tai (the Khamtis being of Tai origin) assimilates with the religious model of Myanmar Theravada faith. The author's personal experiences of travel through the Buddhist sites of Eastern and Northeast India, Nepal and Myanmar, have been cited to explain how, in this vast domain, Buddhist faiths and practices of a diverse nature have intermingled.

Anand Singh's *Engaged Buddhism: Locating Space in the Asian Context* focuses on the Copernicus-Newton-era integrated human progress with scientific inventions that have been identified with incorrigible consumerism, unbridled greed and the insane desire to conquer nature, which started jeopardising its very equilibrium. In the twentieth century the devastating effects of such anthropocentricism could be felt in every walk of human life, which has led to some new approaches to examining the academic and theological interpretations of human relations with nature. The scholars, monks and lay followers engaged in Buddhology are also taking a keen interest in investigating and applying Buddhist doctrines vis-a-vis environmental concerns. This has resulted in a widespread development in Southeast Asia popularly known as 'Engaged Buddhist Movements' in which the methodology and techniques of each nation is different from the others, evolved from local requirements and traditions.

Mamata Desai's essay, *Tibetans in India: Socio-Cultural Adaptation,* focuses on the social life in Tibet which was controlled by the monasteries in accordance with the Tibetan religious order. Even during exile in India, the Tibetan religious-intellectual tradition was preserved through institutions founded and supervised by the Central Tibetan Administration (CTA) in Dharamshala. In this paper, the CTA's role in preserving the traditional Buddhist environment among Tibetan refugees in India has been analysed.

Maya Joshi, in *Rahul Sankrityayana's Engagement with Buddhism: A Multi-Layered Weave* argues that one cannot refer to Buddhist Studies in India without invoking the life and work of Mahapandita Tripitakacharya Rahul Sankrityayana (1897-1963). Also known affectionately as Rahul-ji, this polymath represents a vibrant activism-oriented engagement with India and its past and present, coupled with the spirit of earnest and sustained intellectual inquiry. The paper also traces the complex contours of the extraordinary biographical milestones in Rahul-ji's life in terms of his ceaseless quest for a valid socially transformative set of ideas as well as his parallel academic/scholarly/textual contribution to Buddhist Studies. It places him in his historical context and suggests how his engagement with Buddhism, though at one level almost idiosyncratically unique, may yet be seen as reflecting the spirit of the age.

Madhumita Chattopadhayay's essay, *Concept of Revenue Generation in Buddhist Literature* elucidates the existence of a revenue system, as indicated and reflected in the Buddhist texts, even though sometimes there is no mention of any clear-cut principle for a tax system. In an attempt to analyse and substantiate her argument the author refers to *Aggañña Sutta* of the *Dīgha Nikāya* and many other sources of Buddhist literature. In *Aggañña Sutta* it is stated that when the people decided to select from among themselves a person to look after their fields so that the crops were not stolen, a figure whom they regarded as *mahājanasammata* or as *rājā*, they planned to offer him one-sixth of the crops generated. Thus, she argues, this text means that they were ready to submit as revenues for the land one-sixth portion of the harvest to the king in lieu of the service they received from him, namely the protection and maintenance of their individual lands. The essay points out that the Buddhist texts give us an idea of the origin of state administration, an account of tax submission, the importance of revenue earning for maintenance of a state, methods of tax collection and the status of two officers, namely *rajjuguhaka-amacca* and *dronaamapa-kamahamatta,* responsible for land-revenue collection; and various forms and sources of revenue generation, such as, land revenue, property tax, taxes and duties related to trade and commerce, gate-tax, customs-frontier, toll-tax etc.

Bela Bhattacharya, in her essay *Pali and Buddhist Studies in India—A Brief Survey* examines how the Pali *bhasa* (language) is a comparatively modern coinage. Doubtful whether the term Pali as a language was coined by the European orientalists or the Theras of Ceylon, she is certain that it is not before 6$^{th}$ or 7$^{th}$ century A.D. that the nomenclature Pali came into use for the language of the texts of the cannon of the Theravada Buddhists; the term Pali in the sense of the original texts of the Tipitaka synonymous with Buddhavacana. The Buddha preached his religion, doctrine and discipline for forty-five years in different Janapadas—Kasi, Kosala, Anga, Magadha, Kuru etc. After the Buddha's Mahaparinibbana his disciples collected his sayings, collectively called Buddhavacana, i.e. 'words of the Buddha'.

Ravindra Panth in his *Potentials of Buddhist Studies with Special Reference to Pali Literature* discusses the special relevance of Buddhist Studies today, quoting Einstein on how Buddhism is the religion of the future. In order to bring the development process into harmony with our inner identity and the building of character, attention must shift to issues that help in making a human being humane. Buddhist Studies encompasses the philosophy of life, being directly concerned with the well-being of humanity and fully capable of guiding the people to mitigate their suffering.

Sristidhar Dutta, in his essay *Living Buddhism in Arunachal Pradesh: An Assessment*, refers to Northeast India as an ethnographic paradise, the meeting ground of diverse cultures since the prehistoric period, where one can notice the flourishing of various formal and informal religious faiths, beliefs and ideas. Buddhism is one among these which has considerably influenced the life and culture of various indigenous groups of the area. In Arunachal Pradesh, we notice both the living traditions of Buddhism—Theravada and Tibetan Lamaism. The Buddhist cultural heritage of the state is reflected in more than a hundred Buddhist monasteries, repositories of fine arts and mural paintings, stupas, manuscripts and manuscript paintings, colourful monastic dances and festivals and oral traditions.

Thus, Buddhist heritage is an important aspect of the Arunachali culture. Buddhism played an important role in the socio-economic and politico-cultural life of the people of the state. The ethnic, cultural and historic as well as border trade relationship of the Buddhist people of Arunachal Pradesh can play a vital role in the furtherance and implementation of the Look East policy initiated by the Government of India.

Lalit Shyam writes on *Living Buddhism in Assam—A Vibrant Force in Flourishing Culture and Tradition.* In ancient times Assam was known by different names in different texts: *Pragyotisha* or Pragoytishapura, Kamrupa, Vesali or *Wri-sa-li-long* (Vesali in Buddhist literature) and *Moung-diun-shoun-kham* (the land of the golden garden). Till recent times, the boundaries of greater Assam included Arunachal Pradesh, Nagaland, Meghalaya, Mizoram, Tripura and Manipur. Living Buddhism in Assam, as being professed and practised by the Tai people and some other tribal communities, can be divided broadly into two schools, namely the southern school of Buddhism or orthodox tradition of Buddhism, Theravada and Northern school of Buddhism or Mahayana Buddhism. His essay focuses on different aspects of such living traditions of the Buddhist communities in Assam.

## Way Forward

The Institute envisages a long-term project seeking to understand the Buddhist cultural links across various regions of Asia. Scholars, reporters, photographers, artists, businessmen and cultural enthusiasts within and outside India are expected to participate in this MAKAIAS initiative. Visits to various Buddhist sites within India (e.g. Sanchi, Sarnath, Bodhgaya, Nalanda, Sravasti, Dharamsala, Spiti, Kinnaur, Amaravati, Ladakh, Dharamsala, Pemyangtse monastery in Sikkim, Ajanta and Ellora caves, Tawang and other important sites in North East India and many more) are to be prioritised. An annual journal on *Buddhism in Asia,* supervised by an editorial board comprising of experts on the subject, reports based on international conferences and India-based workshops and interactive meetings should be introduced within this period. Linkages with Mahabodhi Societies across India would be explored. Documentation centres and repositories in South Asia (India, Bangladesh, Sri Lanka), South East Asia (Myanmar, Cambodia, Thailand, Vietnam, Singapore), Asiatic Russia (Buryatia), Mongolia and East Asia (China, Japan, South Korea) with their corpus of literature on Buddhism, could be consulted, and a Directory of material on transnational Buddhism could be drawn up. The project is at an initial exploratory stage; this seminar just an introductory initiative. A more detailed note on the project follows.

**Sreeradha Datta**

# PILOT PROJECT ON 'TRAILING BUDDHISM IN ASIA': A NOTE

While Indian universities like Gautam Buddha, Nava Nalanda Mahavihara, Nalanda and several other universities, institutes and organisations in different parts of India are engaged in various programmes and courses related to Buddhism, there is limited knowledge both within India and outside of the studies being undertaken.

The goal of the pilot project is to bridge this gap.

The initial objective is to prepare a directory providing an overview of the Buddhist Studies courses in India. With this, MAKAIAS is attempting to build a connection with India's immediate neighbours in which Buddhism is an integral part of life, and where one sees a tremendous vibrancy around Buddhism in recent times.

This Directory is intended to contain a comprehensive list of the institutes, organisations and universities all over India engaged with the study of Buddhism. This will cover the various programmes related to the study of Buddhism that are being conducted; the courses and curricula being offered to students; projects for postgraduate courses such as M.Phil, PhD being undertaken or submitted; and the areas they are focusing on.

In connection with the objectives mentioned above MAKAIAS

initially engaged with other institutions and universities of India. All participants teaching such courses were requested to share their information and databases from courses or projects underway at their institutes or universities, including brief information about the course, curriculum, projects undertaken or submitted, and future plans. This would help MAKAIAS draw up an inclusive database of the actual number of Indian Universities or Institutes engaged with the study of various aspects of Buddhism. This database first helped identify the nature of the programmes that are current and active. Identifying this in the large number of Universities/Institutes spread all over India would be a useful exercise towards understanding the scope and future possibilities of making this a far more dynamic study that would draw the attention of a much larger audience. The study will then also be able to both throw light on those aspects that are being given greater salience and ascertain the gaps that may exist.

Another object of this endeavour is to cohesively link up the on-going individual Buddhism-related projects being pursued by the Fellows of MAKAIAS (particularly those connected to Northeast India where Buddhism is a living tradition and practice) with similar projects undertaken by different institutes, organisations and universities across India, and at a later stage, as declared at the BCIM Forum, with neighbouring countries of India.

The Buddhist influence in Northeast India has not necessarily come only from within India; many other countries, like China, Thailand, and Japan amongst others, have had an influence in the region, the importance of which cannot be ignored by MAKAIAS as an institute working on International affairs. Moreover, Buddhism is to be seen not only in terms of architecture, archaeology, music, etc. but also in terms of the significant soft-power potential it holds in the contemporary world.

Thus, the whole idea behind this particular project *Trailing Buddhism in Asia* is to introduce and share context; to perceive the overall philosophy, the common idea that percolates through different strands of Buddhism in Asia; how Buddhism is being shaped or diluted in different Asian countries like Sri Lanka, Bangladesh, Thailand or Asiatic Russia, eventually stretching to include West, Southeast and the northern reaches of Asia.

We hope to embark on the following collaborative initiatives:

- To share the experience of teaching Buddhist studies at their respective universities/institutes/organisations by participants.
- To brainstorm and ideate on how the scholars of MAKAIAS and other universities/institutes/organisations engaged in Buddhism Studies can interact and work together on a sustained basis to ensure that in five years' time it would be possible to produce something which has not been attempted before in India.
- Every six months to jointly take stock of where this particular project stands and to discuss how to go ahead with it.
- To discuss and identify probable constraints in the tightly controlled course curriculum of the universities/institutes where MAKAIAS as a research institute can come in.
- To chart out how cohesively this project can be handled with MAKAIAS, given its resources, and the different projects undertaken by its scholars.
- To trace the lacunae in this particular area and endeavour to address them first from within and then beyond the country.
- To engage in foreign collaborations as has been very successfully achieved by Nalanda University.

We wish to make this MAKAIAS project—*Trailing Buddhism in Asia*—useful not only to those who seek to study Buddhism but also to those who would like to examine the issue through a socio-political prism or an academic lens.

**Sreeradha Datta**
Director, MAKAIAS

# ARTICLES

# 1

# Buddhist Studies in India: A Vital Link for Peace and Prosperity in the Asian Countries

*Ram Nandan Singh*

## Introduction

Buddhism is completely compatible with the modern age, and it has all the qualities, characteristics and traits towards the concept of achieving, providing and sustaining peace and prosperity in the Asian countries in particular and in the whole world in general. That is why Albert Einstein opines, "The religion of the future will be a cosmic religion. It will transcend a personal God and avoid dogmas and theology. Covering both the natural and spiritual it should be based on a religious sense arising from all things—natural and spiritual as a meaningful unity. Buddhism answers this description."

The phrase "Buddhist Studies" is an academic nomenclature and used in academic parlance. It is an established fact that "Buddhist Studies" stands for Buddhism in toto.

It is a historical testimony that Buddhism has been a reigning religion and a practicing faith in Asian countries since the third century BCE. According to the *Mahavamsa, Ashokavadana, Avadanakalpalata*, and sundry other authentic sources, Emperor Ashoka got Buddhism introduced and propagated it far and wide. The archaic text *Mahavamsa* clearly informs that the Buddhist missionaries were dispatched to nine different regions and countries, as Maharakkhita was sent to Yona, i.e., the modern Bactrian and Greek regions, Majjhima to the Himalayan regions, Sona and Uttara to Suvarnabhumi, modern Myanmar, Mahinda to Lanka and so on.

In fact, Buddhism is rooted in the Asian countries in the form of both Theravada Buddhism and Mahayana Buddhism. Theravada Buddhism is prevalent to the south of India, viz. Sri Lanka, Myanmar, Indonesia, Thailand, Indo-China (Vietnam, Cambodia, Laos), and so on. Furthermore, Mahayana Buddhism is present to the north of India, such as Tibet, Central Asia (Uzbekistan, Tajikistan, Kirgizia, Armenia, et cetera), Baltic regions (Latvia, Lithuania, Estonia), China, Mongolia, Korean peninsula, the Far East, Japan and so forth. In this way, Buddhism can play a vital role in achieving, providing and sustaining peace and prosperity in the Asian countries.

The principles and doctrines of Buddhism are in congruence with paradigms of modern social moves and dynamics, political thoughts and ideals, philosophical underpinnings both in epistemological and ontological terms, economical perceptions based on the Middle Path of Buddhism, and ecumenical notions as well as syncretism of Mahayana Buddhism in the framework of Buddhayana. Thus, all these principles and doctrines of Buddhism lead towards peace and prosperity in the modern world.

The sermons and discourses of Gautama Buddha are based on scientific notion. Mention may be made of the *Kalama Sutta* of the *Anguttara Nikaya*, which is regarded as the "Charter of Free Inquiry". In fact, the edifice of Buddhism is rooted in pragmatic realism and experimentation, that is to say, science. The Buddha exhorts in the *Tattvasangraha* of Santaraksita as, "O Monks! Do not accept my word as true out of reverence. Accept my words as true only after examination just as gold is accepted as true only after heating, piercing and rubbing." This sort of Buddhist concept leads towards peace and prosperity based on scientific temper and pragmatic realism.

In this paper, let me begin by proposing a thesis that could considerably conceptualise "Buddhist Studies in India" in the paradigm of achieving and sustaining peace and prosperity in the Asian countries in accordance with the Buddhist principles and doctrines in the modern age.

It is high time to talk about peace and harmony in the world. The changing scenario of the world has pushed society and humanity to the brink of war and catastrophe. The world is sitting on the powder-keg. It may explode anytime and anywhere in the world. There are weapons of mass destructions in the form of chemical, biological, nuclear war heads, and so on. The war perceptions, hostilities and terrorism have not ceased even after coming of a unipolar world. It is truism that the cold war of the bipolar world has come to an end, but it has given rise to the one-manship, and overwhelming power for policing the entire world. So, once again the casualty is world peace.

In this dispensation, Buddhism can play a decisive role for providing, sustaining and preserving peace and harmony in the Asian countries in particular and in the world in general. The religion of *Shakyamuni* Gautama Buddha is totally compatible with the notion of achieving, providing and sustaining peace and prosperity in the society.

The tenets, doctrines and philosophy of Buddhism are best suited for inter-faith dialogue, harmony and universal peace. It is a historical fact that Buddhism has been a reigning religion in the entire East-Asia, South East Asia, Central Asia, and South Asia. Even today, Buddhism can resurrect the universal brotherhood, peaceful co-existence, harmonious surroundings and, of course, peace and prosperity in the comity of nations. This can be done by invoking the salient features and characteristics of Buddhism.

In this background, there are salient characteristics of Buddhism, which have been contributing to peace and prosperity since its inception.

## Buddhist Theory of Interdependence

Buddhism enjoins the adoption of interdependence. This metaphysical concept is known as "*Pratityasamutpada*",[1] that is to say, "The Doctrine of Dependent Origination" in the Buddhistic parlance. According to the afore-noted concept, everything is relative in the universe and nothing is permanent. In a nutshell, every entity of this universe should live in a peaceful co-existence manner primarily because every entity is interdependent. This is a unique concept, perhaps exclusive one of Buddhism.

The Doctrine of Dependent Origination is the foundation of all the teachings of Gautama Buddha. The Second Noble Truth and the Third Noble Truth constitute the Doctrine of Dependent Origination. The Second Noble Truth connotes the cause of sufferings and the Third Noble Truth gives the annihilation of sufferings. The concept of *Pratityasamutpada* may be analysed on the basis of scientific methodology. This doctrine is based on the theory of causality.[2] It means everything is relative and nothing is permanent.

The great twentieth century scientist Albert Einstein also propounded the Theory of Relativity, which is totally in agreement with the Doctrine of Dependent Origination. In short, nothing is permanent in this universe. Conversely, everything is relative. This is the essence of teachings of Gautama Buddha. By implication, every person, society, country, continent and so on are interdependent.

Further, there is a symbiotic relationship amongst human beings, plants and earth. It is a scientific fact that human beings and animals inhale oxygen and exhale carbon dioxide, whereas plants inhale carbon dioxide and exhale oxygen in a diurnal ambience. In short, there is an interdependence between man and plants. This natural phenomenon is completely compatible to the Doctrine of Dependent Origination, that is to say, *Pratityasamutpada*, which can play a vital role in achieving, providing and sustaining peace and prosperity in the Asian countries.

## Buddhist Doctrine of Ahimsa

*Ahimsa*[3] implies refraining from killings of living beings. Man, animals and plants are living beings. So, how can a follower of *Ahimsa* destroy a living being? Moreover, *Ahimsa* has been accorded utmost importance in Buddhism. In the *Catuhasataka* of Aryadeva, it is stated that *Tathagata* has enunciated *Dharma* in the paradigm of *Ahimsa*. The *Catuhasataka*[4] explicates: "*Dharma samasatoahimsa varnayanti Tathagatah*". Thus, *Ahimsa* advocates for peace and prosperity.

## Buddhist Welfare Thought of Brahmavihara

*Brahmavihara* is the forerunner of peace and prosperity. It is contingent upon the *Bodhicitta*. The etymological meaning of the term '*Bodhicitta*' is the enlightened mind. It facilitates for possession of *Brahmavihara*. It acts like a springboard. *Bodhicitta* is also related to the consciousness. The early Buddhist philosophy is a psycho-ethical analysis of the consciousness. The consciousness is the hub of every action. In this regard, Gautama Buddha exhorts in the *Anguttara Nikaya* of the *Sutta Pitaka* as:[5]

"*Cetana aham, Bhikkhave, kammam vadami*"
(That is to say: O Monks! Consciousness is the volition.)

*Brahmavihara* is directly related to the consciousness, which is again related to ethics. The right consciousness leads to right action and the wrong consciousness paves the way for wrong action. Ethics has got a very important place in Buddhism. Gautama Buddha has summarised entire Buddhism on the basis of ethics in a couplet, which runs as below:[6]

"*Sabba papassa akaranam, kusalassa upasampadas*
*Sacittapariyodapanam, etam Buddhana sasanam*"
(That is to say: Abstaining from all sorts of sin, doing good to all living beings, and making one's mind pure is the Buddhadharma.)

*Bodhicitta* is necessary for *Brahmavihara*. *Bodhicitta* is always positive. It annihilates I-ness and egoistic dispensation which stands for desire of holding power to control over man and material on the earth. When *Bodhicitta* is attained, *Brahmavihara* is established, and then the peace and prosperity is metamorphosed.

In this context, the Kalinga war of Emperor Ashoka may be cited as related to *Metta Brahmavihara*. According to the Thirteenth Rock Edict,[7] King Ashoka adopted '*Dhammaghosa*', which is to say, the sound of Righteousness instead of '*Bherighosa*', that is to say, the sound of trumpet after having seen the huge destructions of men, animals and materials during the Kalinga war. Thus, the adoption of '*Dhammaghosa*' was effected only when King Ashoka got attracted towards the *Dhamma* of Gautama Buddha and by implication the attainment of *Brahmavihara* by the Emperor Ashoka. As a consequence, the culture of non-violence was introduced to the Indian culture in regard to statecraft and polity. As corollary, peace and prosperity was achieved.

## Buddhist Rationalistic Thought

Gautama Buddha did not propagate any gospel and dogma. The entire corpus of teachings and sermons of the Buddha is based on pragmatic realism and rational thinking. Gautama Buddha exhorted, "*Atta dipa viharatha.*" (That is to say: Be light unto yourself). He further states in the *Attavagga* of the *Dhammapada* by the following way:[8]

> "*Atta hi attano natho ko hi natho parosiya*"
> (That is to say: A man is his Lord himself, not someone else)

The point is that when rational thinking prevails, the formation of culture comes to the fore automatically. Gautama Buddha provided a full-fledged freedom to think, decide and act. He did not thrust any ideas upon his followers in any form. The *Tattvasangraha* of Acarya Santarakshita states it in a crystal clear way:[9]

> "*Tapacchedacca nikasat suvarnamiva panditaih*
> *Pariksya, Bhiksavo, grahyam madvaco na tu gauravat*"
>
> (That is to say: O Monks, my words should be accepted by the wise, not out of regard for me, but after due investigation, just as gold is accepted as true only after heating, cutting and rubbing).

Thus, the rationalistic thought based on individualistic freedom in accordance with Buddhism paves the way for peace and prosperity.

## Buddhist Democratic Thought

Gautama Buddha is the first person in the world who established his Order known as the *Buddhist Sangha* based on democratic thought and republican ideas. *Sangha* was regulated by the *Patimokkha*. On the basis of an analogy between the *Patimokkha* of Gautama Buddha and modern day sundry constitutions of the world, it will be evident that the *Buddhist Sangha* was constituted strictly in line with the democratic ideals and thinking. In the *Patimokkha,*[10] the *Parajika Dhamma*, four in numbers are unjustifiable like the

Fundamental Rights in the Indian Constitution, which are unjustifiable but have precedence over the Directive Principle of State Policy. In this way, the contribution of Buddhism to the Indian jurisprudence on the basis of democratic thoughts and ideals is peerless. Thus, all these actions both tangible and intangible paved the way for peace and prosperity.

## Welfare and Culture

The Buddhist concept of welfare is well-known. In the *Mahavagga*, Gautama Buddha exhorts as the following:[11]

> *"Caratha, Bhikkhave, carikam bahujana hitaya, bahujana sukhaya, lokanukampaya atthaya hitaya devamanussanam'ti"*

Gautama Buddha rejected the caste system based on birth, and adopted the theory of *Karma* as stated in the *Vasalasutta* of the *Suttanipata* which runs as follows:[12]

> *"Na jacca vasalo hoti, na jacca hoti brahmano?*
> *Kammuna vasalo hoti, kammuna hoti brahmano"*

The Buddha accorded utmost importance to wisdom and conduct. instead of one's lineage. The relevant couplet of the *Ambatthasutta* of the *Digha Nikaya* states as:[13]

> *"Khattiyo settho janetasmin ye gotta patisarino*
> *Vijjacarana sampanno so settho devamanusei'ti"*

Thus, these ideas and thoughts are universal in nature and help forming cultural accumulation, which contribute to achieving, providing, and sustaining peace and prosperity.

## Buddhist Political Thought

The political thought of Buddhism is very prominent, conducive and helpful for the modern world in regard to peace and prosperity. The political thought of Gautama Buddha as regards the governance of state was delivered when Ajatasatru, the king of Magadha, was determined to attack the *Vajjians* of Vaisali. As a consequence, the Buddha formulated the "Seven Fold Policy of State Welfare." It is stated in the *Mahaparinibbanasutta* of the *Digha Nikaya.* This sort of political thought has immensely contributed to the peace and prosperity.

The tenets, doctrines and philosophy of Buddhism have unambiguously contributed to the peace and prosperity.

Finally, the Buddhist Studies itself can be a vital link for achieving, providing and sustaining peace and prosperity in the Asian countries in particular and to the entire world in general.

## NOTES

1. Shastri, Shantibhikshu (tr.), *Lalitavistara*, 1st ed., Lucknow: Uttar Pradesh Hindi Sansthan, 1984, pp. 786-7.
2. Bapat, P.V. (ed.), *2500 Years of Buddhism*, Leh: Mahabodhi International Meditation Centre, 1996, p. 29.
3. Basham, A.L., *The Wonder That Was India*, 3rd rev. ed., New Delhi: Rupa & Co., 2001, p. 285.
4. Quoted in Shastri, Shantibhikshu (tr.), *Bodhicaryavatara*, 2nd ed., Lucknow: Buddha Vihar Risaldar Park, 1983, p. 44.
5. Quoted in Revatadhamma, B. and Tripathy, R. (eds.), *Abhidhammatthasangaho,* Part I, Varanasi: Varanaseya Sanskrit Visvavidyalaya, 1967, p. 32.
6. Singh, S. (tr.), *Dhammapada*, Delhi: University of Delhi, 1977, p. 32.
7. Bapat, P.V. (ed.), *2500 Years of Buddhism,* Leh: Mahabodhi International Meditation Centre, 1996, P. 56.
8. Singh, S. (tr.), *op. cit.*, p. 30.
9. Sastri, Swami D. (ed.), *Tattvasangraha*, 2nd ed., Varanasi: Baudha Bharati, 1982, Volume 3587, p. 1115.
10. Sastri, Swami D. (ed.), *Patimokkhasutta,* Varanasi: Baudha Bharati, 1981, pp. 4-6.
11. Tiwary, M. (ed.), *Mahavaggo*, Delhi: University of Delhi, 1982, p. 29.
12. Dharmaraksita, B. (ed. and tr.), *Suttanipata,* Delhi: Motilal Banarsidass, 1995, p.34.
13. Tiwary, M. (ed.), *Digha Nikaya*, Delhi: University of Delhi, 1982, p. 29.

# 2

# Regional Representation of Myanmar Buddhism in Northern, Eastern and North Eastern India

*Swapna Bhattacharya (Chakraborti)*

## Introduction

The paper has addressed issues relating to India-Myanmar relations, within the framework of Buddhism and Buddhist Studies. In the past, Myanmar and India constituted a single cultural realm: vast, complex, unorthodox and all-pervading. In both the countries, Islam and Christianity were indigenised in India whereas Hinduism and Buddhism shared the same umbilical cord. It is because of the sense of tolerance and inner wisdom of the Hindus and the Buddhists that religious syncretism became a way of life in India and Myanmar. One would be familiar with this author's argument about coming together of Vaishnavism, Sufism and Buddhism. It was not because of political compulsion but because of the *Panna* (Prajna: wisdom) of the majority of the people of India and Myanmar which made this peaceful co-existence possible. The author's field visits to

Myanmar (about seven times in the last twenty years) have been accompanied by a number of major archaeological site visits in Pagan, Mandalay, Prome, Pegu. Equally inspiring were visits to many edifices of Indian origin that bear the stamp of cultural commonness between Myanmar and India. My journeys across Myanmar have inspired me to trace the legacy of cultural intercourse as existed in our land. This inspired me to visit places of pilgrimage in Bodhgaya, Nalanda, Vesali, Sravasti, Benares, Rajagriha, Kushinagar, Lumbini which were destinations for millions of Myanmar people over thousands of years. The Myanmar cultural model has its impact in various parts of Assam and north eastern states of India. The "Myanmar cultural model", in my understanding is not just material culture (weaving, basketry, metal works etc) but also the language, Theravada Buddhism of Myanmar and Buddhist kinship structure. This quest led me to Arunachal Pradesh, especially in Namsai-Chongkham area. Such journeys inspired me further to probe into the Indian scholarly links in Myanmar—whether they were Buddhists or Hindus—whoever realized the importance of Myanmar in the world of Buddhism. The Four Noble Truths, the Eight Fold Path and the concept of *Anicca* (impermanence), *Dukkha* (suffering), *Anatta* (Soullessness) are known to us; in contrast, little known is the fact that between the *kammatic* and *nibbanic* Buddhism there is a third space, to which Melford Spiro referred to in his book.[1] This space between (or beyond?) two normative soteriological schools is occupied by many folkloristic ideas, esoteric, apotropaic practices, parallels of which are found in Bengal, Nepal, Assam and the Himalayan regions. People have been worshipping spirits, minor gods and goddesses or spiritual personalities to ward off the evils, and believed in the advent of the millennium. Spiro seems to suggest that Indian, Chinese, and indigenous beliefs "with an overlay of Buddhist doctrines", for the sake of popular legitimacy, got "loosely integrated" in Myanmar. This is most normal, as Myanmar became the cradle on which the *Kula* (Indic) people and *China* (Sinitic) people came together[2] and enriched themselves, as nowhere else in the region of South and Southeast Asia.

My lessons in Pali and Buddhism with eminent Buddhist scholars in India and Germany have given me enough scope and knowledge about a comparative study. It is almost unquestionable that Myanmar is the country where Buddhism is its purest and pristine form and is unique due to the following factors: first, unbroken tradition, second, dominance of *Abhidhamma* tradition, third, writings of treatises and copying of manuscripts, and fourth, close contacts between the monastic order and the laity. It was due to this last-mentioned factor that the Pongyi movement of the early three decades of the 20$^{th}$ century led by monks (Pongyi) touched the grass root level and even inspired the Indian nationalists to work together for the cause of *nibbana*, i.e., the end of colonial rule.

The name of U Ottama (1894-1939), who was for generations revered as the friendly link between India and Myanmar, comes to light. While my book[3] describes such related stories, in this article I have undertaken the task of breaking new ground. Another area that will be explored is the close link existing between Bengal and Myanmar. In the ongoing discussion, the readers might be taken to a new world of thought in which we witness the patronage of western scholars and the ongoing cooperation between Indian, Myanmar and western scholars to the cause of promotion of Pali and Buddhist Studies.

## I

## Myanmar-India intellectual Continuum: Images, structures, scripts, scholars and cults

The paper argues that the Indian people and the Myanmar people are descendants of a single heritage and civilization, but have been driven apart due to various reasons that are of purely political nature.

British colonial rule during 19th-20th centuries culminated in the unnatural attachment of the British-Indian Empire with the annexed Burmese Empire in 1885-86. This did both the people a great damage. Many senior scholars in Myanmar frankly confessed that the difference arose only when the Indians worked as agents of the colonial rulers. People of both the countries have made efforts to quickly overcome this situation. Scholars and pilgrims visited each other's countries during the 1950s. A vibrant Indian population in various cities of Myanmar (Yangon, Mandalay, Moulmein Sittwe etc) continued to play an important and active role. The Bengalis based in Yangon in particular, very enthusiastically continued with their cultural activities, observing among other occasions, Gurudev Rabindranath Tagore's birthday with their Myanmar counterparts. Professors from Calcutta University went to Yangon, to teach Pali and Buddhism, Indian history among other subjects. They also learnt techniques of meditation, for which Myanmar has won her own place in the Buddhist world.[4]

It is no wonder that a great majority of Myanmar people actually look at India as a country with which they have shared common historical experiences over thousands of years. In a recently published article, eminent historian and a leading intellectual in Myanmar, Professor Khin Maung Nyunt has reminded us that Myanmar and India share a historical civilizational link, believe in same values of freedom against colonial rule. The kings and their families sent emissaries to Benares, Bodhgaya, Bengal and other places to collect texts in Sanskrit. Also, the learned Brahmans were invited to translate the texts to Myanmari language. The *Bhagvad Gita* was read at the court of the king Bodawpaya. As M. Charney rightly states, the South Asian intellectual tradition at the court of the emperor Bodawpaya (1781-1819) was represented by the sacred Hindu writings from India and Pali texts from Sri Lanka.[5] Very little is studied about the different version of the story, where the Buddhist Khamtis or Buddhist Marmas carried back manuscripts of Buddhist scriptures whenever they crossed the border.[6]

More visible are the architectural style, mostly replicas of Shwedagon Pagoda in India, correspondingly replicas of Mahabodhi Temple in Myanmar, in Pagan or even in the premises of the Shwedagon Pagoda in Yangon. Unknown to the anthropologists of India is the fact that kinship terminologies in so called tribal societies of North Eastern India and South Eastern Bangladesh are of Myanmar origin. One such example is the Myanmar word, *Amyo*, which means "blood relation" or simply "kinship".[7] Indian literature, like *Dharmashastra* of Manu (*Manu Dhammathat*), *Ramayana* and *Jatakas* travelled to Myanmar through Indian merchants, astrologers, Brahmins and cultural adventurers of all kinds. After all, the Pyu (Sinitic origin with Indian faiths) dominated Upper Myanmar was the *Brahmadesh*, the domain of Lord Brahma.[8] While we have lost much of this treasure, people of Myanmar have kept them alive with great care through generations. The Myanmar script goes back to its South Indian origin, the Pallava script. This is most natural, as in the early years of Christian era coastal trade between the South Indian people (for example, the Satavahanas) and the Mons (earlier called Talaings) was actively maintained. Myanmar archaeologists and art historians have no hesitation to acknowledge that all classical styles of art, Amaravati, Gupta, Pala-Sena have their influence upon objects of art and architecture, unearthed across Myanmar, in various parts starting from the border with China down to the border of Bangladesh, in the Rakhine State.[9] The script which went from coastal India came back to the soil of South Asia; for example, the script of the Chakmas of Chittagong Hill Tracts has Myanmar origins. The Khamtis too owe their script to the Shan-Myanmar origin. Another example of a cultural-linguistic connection is the Mahamuni Cult of the Rakhines (Arakanese). As we know along with Golden Rock, Shwdagon, the Mahamuni image (now in Mandalay, but originally from the Rakhine state) make the three major Buddhist assets of Myanmar. As was shown by me through earlier writings, the Mahamuni cult of Rakhine origin also travelled to the Chittagong Hill Tracts as it did to Assam.[10] The Rakhine king Chandrasuriya invited the Lord Buddha to visit Arakan. To avoid the hazards of the long journey from Sravasti, it is believed that the Buddha flew with 500 disciples and landed at Selagiri, opposite Kyauktaw. A sacred image was constructed by Indra and Visvakarma. The Buddha brought life in to the image which became from then onwards His own. This Mahamuni image thus became the symbol of Buddhist royal cult, gave the Arakanese kings legitimacy to rule. It became such a great symbol that the Rakhines kept it with great care, while the Mranma (Burmans) kings constantly tried to capture the image. Ultimately, king Bodawpaya annexed Arakan in 1784 and took away the Mahamuni image, and placed it in his new capital, Mandalay. In 2012, I had the privilege to have a *darshan* of Mahamuni in the Mahamuni Pagoda, Mandalay.

The Mans of Meghalaya practice Buddhism of the Theravada school.[11] The term *Mans* come quite close to *Mons* of Myanmar. There is little doubt that the Mans are the co-brethren of the Mons of Lower Myanmar, who were under the constant pressure from the Mranma people (from China including Tibet) who came down in various splinter groups to occupy the fertile river valleys of Irrawaddy, Chindwin, Kaladan in Myanmar and Brahmaputra in India. According to Singh, the Mans worship Lakshmi, Saraswati, yet observe Buddhist norm of following *Panch-Sheel* (abstinence from five vices) and *Asta Sheel* (eight principles). The images of Lord Buddha, which the Mans worship have Yogic posture. This is quite interesting in the context of the fact that Yogis were numerous in this entire region, from Assam, Tripura to upper Myanmar. This is why Spiro goes on to argue that the alchemists called Zawgyi are "the Burmese corruption of Yogi".[12] Though Theravada in essence, Myanmar Buddhism co-opted several Mahayana beliefs and practices.[13] This came in the wake of the immigration of Indian merchants and travellers who lived in ancient Myanmar and enjoyed social prestige. Thus, one should not be surprised to see the paintings having Tantric influence in the Nandamanna and Payathonzu temples of Pagan. Lama Taranatha, the 16th century Buddhist monk of Tibetan origin stated that Mahayana belief flourished in the Kokiland, which included Pukham (Pagan), Rakhan (Arakan) and Hamsavati (Pegu). The name "Koki" can be placed in parallel with the ethnic term "Kuki" of modern Assam and north eastern region.

The British administrators excluded these frontier areas (CHT, Assam, North East India) to make a buffer zone between the Myanmar Empire of the Kongbaung dynasty and the British Indian Empire, based in Bengal. Although, the British ethnographers and administrators have left a rich legacy upon which the anthropology of modern India has been founded, yet, none of them showed any interest to study remnants of Buddhism in what they called "tribal" society. The usage of the term "tribal" is more acceptable given the dichotomy and axiomatic notions of religious affiliations like Hinduism or Buddhism. In the post-independence period, most of the Indian anthropologists, historians and social scientists tend to follow this model of tribal-non tribal distinction. In Myanmar, such a trend was traditionally followed in the domain of Pali studies and in the form of engaged Buddhism. Very recently, Pali studies in Sri Lanka attracted more followers than Myanmar. Nevertheless, relations between Myanmar and India have improved in recent years and since then Indian scholars tend to take more interest in their closest neighbour.[14]

## II

## The World of Buddhism: My Journey and Reminiscences

The MAKAIAS (Kolkata) workshop 'Buddhist Studies in India', aims at drawing up some outlines for revised methodology of

Buddhist studies in India, in eastern India, in particular. My suggestion bears memories of my own training. This takes me back a long way. This exercise has given me the opportunity of paying homage to and remembering some of my teachers, who not only taught me Buddhist literature, Pali grammar and Prakrit languages, Myanmar language, but also taught me to ignore worldly miseries through practice of *sila* (virtue), *samadhi* (concentration) and *panna* (wisdom). An interactive workshop of this kind gives scope for sharing of thoughts at an informal level. Here are a few memories of my journey into the domain of Buddhism in general and Myanmar Buddhism in particular. My journey into the world of Buddhism started as early as in 1971 when I selected Sanskrit literature, Pali, Prakrit and Buddhism as my optional papers under the Special Paper Group "Sanskrit Literature," as against Indian Philosophy. That was the time (late 1960s and early 1970s) when the University of Visva Bharati at Santiniketan experienced a renaissance in Pali and Buddhist studies, with Professor Biswanath Banerjee joining as Head of the Post Graduate Department of Sanskrit. I was fortunate to be one of those fortunate students whom he taught Pali language and literature, Sanskrit drama, Prakrit and Buddhist theology. Professor Banerjee represented a rare combination of classical training in India (in Calcutta University) and at the same time western (German) Indology. We, his students were immensely benefited by this combined scholarship, liberal in natural, open and vast. Professor Nalinaksha Dutta, the great name in Buddhist Studies was his teacher. In Santiniketan during late 1960s and early 1970s my engagement with the study of German language and literature ran parallel to my studies with Sanskrit literature. Thus, in between the lectures or at the end of the class, Professor Banerjee shared with me some of his wonderful experiences with German Indologists and Buddhologists. His admiration for Professor P.C Bagchi was quite natural for both teachers belonged to the same school and were not restricted by the narrow limits of orthodoxy. In both their works, Buddhism has been highlighted as a living social force and not a static world of learning. Professor Banerjee had the opportunity to work with Professor Bagchi in Visva Bharai when the former served Visva Bharati in the early 1950s, before he left for Munich. Professor Banerjee's works with his liberal interpretation of Mahayana Buddhism, especially the *Kalacakrayana*, is widely known. He repeatedly emphasised on the syncretic trends within Buddhism and explained the social and political factors which made this possible. In the process of accommodation with grass root society, Buddhism had to indulge in esoteric practices, often called Tantric in nature. Here, he does not distinguish between Hindu Tantra and Buddhist Tantra. Even then, the fact remains that Theravada orthodoxy enjoyed the highest status in Myanmar society. Thus, the strict barrier between Theravada orthodoxy and Mahayana thought remained, while various reforms within the system of Sangha were considered necessary. But, to come back to the more liberal domain to which Banerjee and other scholars referred to—one has to start with the concept of God, not otherwise popular in Buddhism. This feature silently crept into the fold of Buddhist learning whereby *Vajrasattva* was conceived as the Adi Buddha, the primordial God. The assimilation of Hindu deities culminated with the development of the Kalacakra system, the latest phase of Buddhism, as argued by Professor Banerjee. Looking at the Hindu deities and figurines in the archaeological remains of Myanmar, I am often reminded of Professor Banerjee's remarks about "the limits" of Buddhism that people in Myanmar became aware of. In the case of Kalacakra tradition, it entered Tibet through Kashmir in 1026 A.D.[15] Biswanath Banerjee sets Vajrasattva and Kalcakra on the same plane, and brings into view the duality as expressed in *Sunyata* and *Karuna* on the one hand and *Prajna* and *Upaya* on the other. The concept *kala* (time) is entwined with the norms of astrology and astronomy.

Besides Professor Biswanath Banerjee, Dr. Sujit Muherjee and Dr. Madhusadan Mallik introduced me to the world of Pali, Prakrit, linguistics and Buddhism. Professor Mallik was a student of Professor Benimadhav Barooah, one of the greatest Buddhist scholars of modern India. On the other hand, Professor Sujit Mukhopadhyaya, a true Ashramite and a student of Gurudev Tagore, taught us *Avadana* literature, like texts from the *Ashokavadana* and *Divyavadana*. Another teacher at Visva Bharati was Professor Krishna Nath Chatterjee who taught us Sanskrit drama, and not Buddhism per se. Yet, being a student of Professor P.C. Bagchi, he shared his world vision with us. Especially interesting was the way in which he shared his experiences in Shanghai University. Also important was knowledge-sharing with my uncle, Professor Parvati Charan Bhattacharya, who taught in Rabindra Bharati University, Jadavpur University and Burdwan University in the field of Bengali, Sanskrit and Linguistics. His experiences of our University system that stretched from Aden to Yangon were worth listening to. His convictions about Indian classical languages, e.g. Persian and Sanskrit were based on his own knowledge and creative pursuits. He translated works like *Parasya Sahitya Parikrama*, *Bangla Bhasa*, *Meghdut Parichay* and Hala's *Gatha Saptha Sati*. Poet Hala's lyrical work was composed in Prakrit which also has variations (Gandhari, Maharashtrian, Sauraseni, Magadhi, Ardhamagadhi) which in turn gave birth to various regional languages of India. During my interaction with the students and faculty of Dagon University, I saw a great interest among them to learn not only Sanskrit, but also various forms of Prakrit.

As graduate student with text-based and grammar-based training, I was not quite familiar with the sociological perspective of Buddhism. This was the time when my second academic journey began—to increase my knowledge of Buddhism and its cultural linkages. My entry into *Suedasien Institut* (South Asia Institute) of Heidelberg University with Professor Hermann Kulke as my Ph.D. supervisor introduced me to the world of living Buddhism. Not only did this encourage me to read Max Weber's writings on Buddhism while my own doctoral thesis was on early medieval Bengal (5$^{th}$ to 13$^{th}$ century A.D.). The comparative approach taught me the significance of studying a period (5$^{th}$-13$^{th}$ centuries) in totality—not only there was a Buddhist timeline but also was there a Hindu-Buddhist syncretic link for understanding the whole of eastern India and even Southeast Asia, particularly Indonesia and Myanmar that could be studied in the context of Bengal's relations with those two countries. I still remember my excitement in reading the Nalanda Inscription of the Pala King Devapala, (843-861 A.D.) in which it was mentioned that King Balaputradeva of Sailendra Dynasty of Srivijaya Empire in Suvarnadvipa (Java-Sumatara) made the formal request to grant the revenue of the five villages towards maintenance of Nalanda Monastery. I was fortunate to have the opportunity to participate in the lectures of Professor Heinz Bechert, yet another great name in the world of Buddhist Studies, especially Buddhism in Sri Lanka and Myanmar. Professor Bechert of Goettingen University and Professor Richard Gombrich of Oxford University edited *The World of Buddhism* in 1996 and it is one of the most reputed books that is in wide circulation in the field of Buddhist studies. Professor Heinz Bechert taught for a semester in Heidelberg at the South Asia Institute on the invitation of Professor Emanuel Sarkisyanz, the celebrated author of *Buddhist background of the Burmese Revolution* written in 1965. Professor Bechert's interest in Bengal's Buddhism and Myanmar-Bengal connections appealed to me tremendously, as I was then involved in learning Myanmar language along with my studies on early medieval Bengal history. Thus, I found Professor Bechert's lectures most educative. Though widely known for his work *Buddhism Staat und Gesellschaft* (1967), his article 'Renaissance of Buddhism in Indonesia' for the journal of the Pali Department of University of Calcutta focussed on the Burmese-Indonesian relations. He is among the few Indologists of Europe who had great admiration for Bengal's Buddhism as well as Bengal's tradition of Buddhist studies. The first international conference on Myanmar was organized by Humboldt University in 1993 and it was a great honour for me to participate in one of its sessions that was chaired by Professor Bechert. My paper on Ari cult of Myanmar—an offshoot of Mahayana-Tantric Buddhism is at the periphery of discourse on religion in Myanmar, especially because of the state's strong affinity to orthodox form of Buddhism. My arguments based on opinions of great scholars like E. Duroisell, Niharranjan Ray and Gordon Luce were appreciated by Professor Bechert. The Pagan-Bengal relationship was intensified during Pala-Sena period not only due to marital ties within the royal families but also due to the fact that there was a constant flow of people from Bengal who found home in Upper Myanmar. This continued and became more intensive with the rise of Islam, while constant patronage by Myanmar kings played a significant role.

Let me come back to yet another chapter of my reminisces: it is from U Tin Htway that I learnt Myanmar (Burmese) words of Pali origin and also the Buddhist background of Myanmar culture as reflected in the language. I developed my deep interest in Myanmar language respect for the Vinayadhara tradition in Myanmar. Let me cite here examples with the two words: *Saya* (Teacher) and *Takatai* (University). The word *Saya* comes from the word Sanskrit *Acharya*. The word *Takatai* on the hand is derived from the name *Takshashila*, the famous Buddhist University which is now within the geographical jurisdiction of Pakistan, but once formed part of the Indic civilization. *Takshashila* (Taxila), like Nalanda in eastern India, flourished as a major centre of learning and knowledge. Buddhism and Buddhist scholarship meant so much for the Myanmar civilization, that a place name became a simple noun. Thus, we see the word *Takshashila* phonetically turned in to *Takatai*. One should also mention that discoveries of Buddhist centers in various parts of India considerably inspired the Myanmar people to look at India for spiritual fulfilment. Thus pilgrimage, even patronised by royal houses, were made; while Bodhgaya remained the major attraction, Sravasti, Rajgriha,

Kushinagara saw constant flow of pilgrims from Myanmar in the 1920s, 1930s, 1940s and 1950s. The pilgrim flow somewhat decreased between 1960s to early 1990s. But, from mid 1990s diplomatic relations improved which helped in the increase of pilgrimage flows between Myanmar and India.

My teaching and research in University of Calcutta Post-Graduate Diploma and M.A. courses on Indonesia and Myanmar have facilitated a good deal of rejuvenation of 'Buddhist studies' too in Bengal which has had the closest contact with these two countries. My classes on Buddhist Resurgence Movement in modern India ($19^{th}$-$20^{th}$ centuries) with special emphasis on the role of individuals, institutions and universities of eastern India and Bengal in particular have had a significant role in the realm of Buddhist studies. Certainly, University of Calcutta stands high in this intellectual tradition, as it was only in this University that a Department of Pali was started in the early years of the $20^{th}$ century. British patronage was spontaneous and came from the high offices based in India. British scholars in University of London were also enthusiatic. Apart from this rather purely academic quest Bengal experienced an unprecedented resurgence of Buddhist identity during $19^{th}$-$20^{th}$ centuries. Institutional support derived from Mahabodhi Society, Bengal Buddhist Association/ Bauddha Dharmankur Sabha, Visva Bharati University became as important as personal initiative of individuals. The Hindu middle class and the Brahmo Samaj affiliates were intensively involved in writing biographies of the Buddha in Bengali, or translating *Dhammapada*s, *Jataka*s or *Avadana*s. The Tagore family of Jorasanko was one of the primary patrons. The spirit of the Mahabodhi movement triggered off by the great Sri Lankan monk Anagarika Dharmapala in the late $18^{th}$ century spontaneously met that of the neo-Vedantic philosophy, preached by Swami Vivekananda. They both shared the same platform in the Parliament of Religions in Chicago in 1991. After the establishment of the Mahabodhi Society in Sri Lanka, a branch of it was established in Kolkata, and the journal *Mahabodhi* was launched in 1893. On the other hand, around the same time the Bengal Buddhist Association was founded by the great monk Kripasarana Mahathera who hailed from Chittagong, but, made Kolkata (Calcutta) his centre of activities. Kripasarana's relation with Buddhists in Myanmar was as deep as his contact with Sri Lanka.

It is amidst this unprecedented spirit of resurgence of an unique identity that one has to understand the fact that a large number of young Myanmar monks and Bengali Buddhist Barooah communities living in Yangon (colonial Rangoon) took initiative to put pressure on the British authorities to start Pali course in Yangon (Rangoon) which was then affiliated to Calcutta University. In 1880 for the first time Pali studies was introduced in the University of Calcutta. It was in Rangoon College that E. Forchammer, the eminent scholar in Myanmar (Burmese) antiquities and an eminent archaeologist who came to Pagan in 1881. It was in Rangoon College (then under Calcutta University) where Pali was introduced for the first time as a subject, as part of the University curriculum. The college Department was separated in 1883 from High School and became full-fledged graduate college. The first Professor of Pali was E. Forchammer. He continued to teach Pali at Rangoon College and was followed by James Gray and Ch. Duroisell and Professor Pe Maung Tin. No other university in India, let alone in Asia, can boast of such a grand tradition of Buddhist and Pali scholarship as the University of Calcutta. Certainly, the patronage extended by Sir Asutosh Mukherjee made it possible. Sir Asutosh Mukherjee, who was appointed as Vice Chancellor of Calcutta University as many as four times by the British authorities patronised classical scholarly work and religious activism. Kripasarana Mahathera, the founder of the Bauddha Dharmankur Sabha (Bengal Buddhist Association) was also another such personality and also the patron of modern reformist movement in Bengal. He was also advisor to Sir Asutosh Mukherjee in matters of Pali Studies at Calcutta University. His *guru,* Punyachara, had strong links with Myanmar and Sri Lanka and thus kept the *guru-sisya parampara* in Bengal that largely thrived on the Myanmar connection, alive.

Ashin Saramedha's (1801-1882) name should be mentioned in this context. He hailed from the Rakhine state of Arakan and came to Chittagong Hill Tracts when the Chakmas of the Hill Tracts needed a reformism of their faith that could save the Theravada order. Saramedha introduced the order which is known as the *Sangharaja Nikaya*. To this day Dharmadut Vihar in Yangon is witness to the age old Arakan-Bengal linkage in Theravada domain. Every Chakma Buddhist, indeed every Buddhist of Bangladesh respectfully remembers Saramedha's contribution in providing a new spirit to the Buddhism of Bengal. My own visit to Dharmadut Vihar in Yangon in 2012 further supplements this data—about the fact that it continues its tradition as the prime centre of the meeting between monks based in Myanmar and those who go from India or Bangladesh to Yangon.

The name of the great monk Ven. Rastrapala Mahathera, founder of the International Meditation Centre, Bodhgaya and founder of the Indian Sangharaja Bhikkhu Mahasabha should also be remembered here. He hailed from a Chittagong Buddhist family and later lived his entire life in India. He became the third Sangharaj of the Mahasabha, which he himself founded. It is interesting to read in the article by Ven. Dr. Barasambodhi Thera,[16] his successor in the International Meditation Centre that Ven. Rastrapala Mahathera went to visit Dharmadut Vihar in 1971. Later on, this great monk was honoured by the Myanmar government with the title *Agramaha Sadharma Jyotikadhvaja*.

*Sayadaws*, as the monks are called in Myanmar, played a great role in the revival of Buddhist identity of Bengal in particular and India in general. During my field trips across Bihar, U.P. and Lumbini, I witnessed the monks' role while living in the Myanmar monasteries especially in Kushinagar and Sravasti. In other places of pilgrimage too, for example, in Bodhgaya, Rajgriha, Pataliputra, Sarnath and

Varanasi, I interacted with the venerable Sayadaws, some of whom have been living in India since 1950s and 1960s. I remember the hospitality that I received from Ven. U Awbatha of the Myanmar monastery in Sravasti, Agga Maha Pandita Sadhamma Jyotikadhaja Ven. Jnanesawar of Kushinagar, Ven. U Nyaneinda and Ven. Sanghabodhi of Bodhgaya. Close to my home in Barasat is a newly founded Myanmar monastery, Bodhisukha, headed by Dr. Nando Ba Tha who explained the significance of Myanmar Buddhism in India. Dr. Ashin Nyanissara popularly known as Sayadaw Sitagu in Myanmar is the founder of Sitagu International Buddhist Academy at Sagaing Hills. The institution is committed to continue the tradition of long established contact between Myanmar and India. The Late Sayadaw U Kavida, the erstwhile Head Monk of the Myanmar Buddhist Monastery (Phongyi Chaung) of Eden Hospital Road in Central Kolkata taught Myanmar Language in Calcutta University's Centre for South & Southeast Asian Studies.

## A. Myanmar Buddhism as a Living Force: Regional Representations in India

In my perception, Myanmar Buddhism due to its *Abhidhamma* tradition, remains a major social force in India. The Abhidhamma tradition is a binding force for Vipassana meditation which is practised in Igatpuri in Maharashtra.[17] U Ottama, U Wisara, U Chandramani and many such Myanmar monks have to be remembered as scholars as well as reformers and also spiritual guides for millions of Indians. In fact, Dr. B.R. Ambedkar was inspired by Myanmar (Burmese) Buddhism and in 1956, in Nagpur, U Chandramani, the oldest living monk in India led the conversion ceremony. The Soni House in Mandalay that hosted Dr. Ambedkar represents what may be referred to as Indo-Myanmar Cultural Continuum. I visited this place in October 2012—to see the revival of Buddha Sasana in India and its expansion in various forms—right from the time of Emperor Ashoka who sent missions to Suvarnadvipa (modern Thaton). Whether it is classical works or whether it is shared lineages—one has to consider works of G. Luce, Duroisell, Emil Forchhammer, Donald Stadtner, Dr. Khin Maung Nyunt, Dr. Nai Pa Hla, Dr. Myint Aung and others. The category "tribal" is biased and needs to be replaced by terms that justify the nomenclature "Indo-Myanmar cultural continuum." Linguistic training scholars of Myanmar should learn Sanskrit; their knowledge in Pali will be extremely beneficial, while in the same way, the Indian anthropologists, art historians or historians in general should learn Myanmar language. I believe they are bound to be fascinated by the exchange of ideas between the Myanmar people and Indian people.

## B. Regional Representation in North Eastern India

Hindu deities are well represented in Myanmar Buddhism. This is not only visible in the works of art and archaeology[18] but has remained a living force in Myanmar society. Donald Stadtner explains that the *vahana* of Goddess Thuraberi, like that of the Hindu goddess Saraswati, is the goose. The deity is seen with "books and manuscripts representing the Tripitaka." The world of 37 Nats (Devas) is nothing but the creation of a long interaction between the people of India and Myanmar. The 37$^{th}$ Nat is the king of all Gods, that is Indra, who is called *Thyagyamin* by the Myanmar people. In most of the pagoda premises you can see in Myanmar devotees are paying their respect not only to Lord Buddha, but also the Devas, the Nats.

In the Introduction of his book *Early Interactions between South and Southeast Asia: Reflections on Cross-Cultural Exchange,* PierreYves Manguin states that in the spread of urban pattern and material culture, the people of Southeast Asia adopted models coming from India. What is more interesting is his other work *Revealing Myanmar's Past: An Anthology of Archaeological Articles.*[19] This book has revived my interest to study the links between undivided

Bengal and Myanmar. What makes the work so unique is Myint Aung's knowledge in Indian art and archaeology with an understanding of Myanmar's position between China and India. His training in archaeology at the Archaeological Survey of India and Deccan College in Pune and his active participation in the excavations in various places of Myanmar like Beikthano (Vishnu city) Halin, Sriksetra, Letpanchibaw, Ayetthema and Winka, Vesali etc along with his unbiased appreciation of the people of ancient Asia has made this book one of the most fascinating works on Asia's archaeology.[20]

The subject of Buddhism practiced by the Khamti community of Arunachal Pradesh (Namsai-Tengapani area) is extremely popular for such comparisons. They have successfully integrated with Indian tradition, upheld their pristine religious model of Myanmar Theravada faith.[21] Their counterparts in Myanmar, Thailand and China have attracted attention of western scholars, but they deserve true attention from the Pali and Buddhist scholars of India. The Singphos have incorporated various indigenous beliefs like the Nat Cult of Myanmar (Hindu Devas) within the broader fold of Buddhism. Let me concentrate on the central role that Myanmar Buddhism played in the life of the Khamti people from Arunachal Pradesh. The Khamtis, as is widely known, are the only people from India's Northeast who have their own script; the script itself is of Tai-Shan origin, but many other Southeast Asian languages (Myanmar, Thai, Cambodian), the script originally went from South India. The scope of the present writing is restricted to the subject of Myanmar legacy in the structural form of the monasteries that have been visited by me during the Pagoda, known as the Golden Pagoda, in Khamti language, Kongmu Kham at Tengapnai in Chongkham village. I had the great privilege and honour to be the guest of Hon'ble Minister Chowna Mein (Minister of Finance, Govt. of Arunachal Pradesh) and his wife Mrs. Sati Nang Mein (Member of the Arunachal Pradesh Assembly). In February, 2010, I had this rare opportunity to take part in the Three

Day long Golden Pagoda Dedication Festival, where 250 Theravada monks from various parts of Eastern and North Eastern India, including Assam and West Bengal. Besides Singhphos, Khamtis, Baruahs, also a large number of Chakmas living in Arunachal Pradesh were assembled there to witness the ceremony, and also to listen to the valuable words of the great monks. Cultural groups and pilgrims from Myanmar also joined their co-brethren. Hon'ble Minister Sree Chowna Mein himself also delivered speeches (Dhamma speeches) which of course I could not follow, as he spoke in Khamti language. I am happy to learn that in 2011 a Tai-Khamti and Singhpho Museum cum Research Centre has been established in the Pali Vidyapith, Chongham. The initiative came, as expected, from Hon'ble Minister Chowna Mein and Ven. Vimalananda Bhikkhu, Secretary, Arunchal Pali Vidyapith. During 2010 I was in the Pali Vidyapith, and was quite impressed by the social welfare oriented activities that the Vidyapith was engaged in, aiming at the youth, so that they could lead a healthy and prosperous life with all their academic dreams once to be fulfilled. Chongkham (Jayanta Sarkar, 1987) once happened to be one of the richest villages of Asia. The prosperity came from the timber industry; for the transportation of timber, elephants were maintained as domestic animals. As logging became a prohibited act, the youth, who never had to bother about any formal career, naturally got a sudden shock, and thus became victims of various social illness. In this challenging social sector the Pali Vidyapith and the monasteries of Chowngham play an immensely important role.

Another great experience was my interaction with Ven. Nyanissara Mahathera. This great Myanmar monk enjoys deep respect from not only the Khamti community of Upper Assam and Arunachal Pradesh, but from all Buddhists across our country. His monastery is situated in a Khamti village in Ledo district of Upper Assam. Like many other Myanmar monks across Bihar and U.P.

(B.P. Barua, 2010) Ven. Gunawantha too, has been living in India for decades now and has become a naturalized Indian citizen.

Going through the quiet and clean roads of Chongkham I was feeling as if I were in a village in Myanmar. In Chongkham I visited the Chownguna Namshum monastery, the World Peace Pagoda and a replica of the great reclining Buddha, which one can see in Pegu in lower Myanmar. There is no doubt that such replicas, the original being in Myanmar, have a special appeal to the local Khamti people, who draw their inspiration from the Myanmar model of Theravada Buddhism. The poor who can hardly afford a trip to Myanmar, tries to achieve their merit (*Punya*) by visiting these and other symbols.

Let me now come to another impressive symbol of Myanmar Buddhism in Arunachal Pradesh. This is in Namsai was not so far from the circuit house where my accommodation was arranged; therefore almost everyday I could visit this Pagoda cum monastery, called Namsai Pariyatti Sasana Buddhist Vihar.[22] For me, most impressive appeared to be the style of the Shwedagon that was followed in the architectural style of the main Pagoda.

The Buddha images, the Bhikkhus and the whole atmosphere inside and outside had a serene effect on me. According to the information provided by B. Tripathy and S. Dutta, the Pariyatti Sasana Monastery was built in 1974-75. The same authors write about other small Buddhist temples in the Namsai. As in the cases of other monasteries that I have seen and written about (in 2010 and 2012), this monastery in Namsai too, has a prayer hall, community hall etc.

My visit in 2010 was restricted to Lohit district only, while a large number of Theravada Buddhist monasteries are there in Changlang district of Arunachal Pradesh.

## Conclusion

The paper has addressed the noble works of resurgence of *Buddhasasana* in India in which generations of Myanmar monks (in Myanmar language called *Sayadaw*) were engaged. It is not enough that the Indian scholars should know the activities of the venerable monks from Bodhgaya—Rajgriha-Nalanda, Benares-Sarnath-Sravasti-Kushinagar who bear the tradition of this age old India-Myanmar relations. Indian scholars should give more attention to the tradition of knowledge sharing, social welfare activities and other missions that the senior Myanmar monks and their associates are extending without any expectation of return in material terms. The study of the holy scriptures (*Pariyatti*) and the revelation of the path leading to salvation (*Patipatti*) are the traditional duties of the monks of Myanmar Theravada order. In India, a large number of Sayadaws deserve our respect for their active engagement in the propagation of Buddhism through numerous meritorious works. For example, a place like Kushinagar could be developed due to selfless service of U Chandramani, the Guru of Dr. Ambedekar, as has been mentioned before. The tradition is being maintained by Ven. Agga Maha Pandita Bhandata Gyaneshwar. The name of Sree Jugal Kishor Birla, a great pioneer of trade, commerce and industry should also be mentioned. Being an earnest worshipper of Lord Buddha he too like U Chandramani contributed a lot to the development of Kushinagar, where Lord Buddha breathed his last. Birla was deeply interest to revive India's relation with Southeast Asia. He offered financial support to Gurudev Tagore, during the latter's visit to Southeast Asia. While the Myanmar monasteries in various parts of India and also in Lumbini (Nepal) are engaged in building up people-to people contact, in a quiet corner of Delhi the Buddhist scholar Shanti Swarup Baudh is busy in writing books, published in Hindi, English, Myanmar and various Indian languages, that introduced Myanmar to the Indian people, India to the Myanmar people and also upholds through his publication, *House Samyak Prakashan*, Dr. B.R.

Ambedkar's mission. Kolkata, a city of writers, editors and publishers could think in similar ways in Bengali, to honour the age old contact between Bengal and Myanmar.

This work is an attempt to pay respect to teachers and scholars and also reflect on the need to rediscover the character of Buddhism as practical by a large section of people in Myanmar as well as eastern and north eastern India. It is worthwhile comparing popular Buddhism in Bengal and Myanmar. The other tradition, i.e. Calcutta University's age old academic contact with Yangon University, through exchange of scholars needs to be reinvigorated. The need is to promote the tradition of Myanmar Buddhism and how that is integrated with Pali scholarship and welfare missions not limited only to the religious people, but by ordinary citizens and the common folk. I would even go to the extent of arguing in favour of ways in which Buddhist tradition has been kept alive in Myanmar the world can learn from Myanmar to keep the Buddhist tradition alive.

## NOTES

1. Melford E. Spiro, *Buddhism and Society: A Great Tradition and its Burmese Vicissitudes*, University of California Press, 1982.
2. S. Bhattacharya, 2014.
3. Swapna Bhattacharya, *India-Myanmar Relations 1886-1948*, Kolkata: K.P. Bugchin & Co., 2007.
4. During one of my recent visits to Yangon University, I could talk to a retired Professor of Pali who happened to be a student of Dr. Debaprosad Guha. Dr. Guha, the great Pali scholar, like Professor Niharranjan Ray, taught at Yangon University during 1950s. They both had immense regard for the city of Yangon and their contribution along with other Indian professors' is remembered with great warmth. One of the names is certainly Professor W.S. Desai, who taught History at Yangon University and has left many students, with whom I had the chance to interact during my conference visits to the country. I only feel sorry that I had no chance to convey this message of India-Myanmar *Guru-sisyaparampara* tradition to Dr. Guha, for he had left this mortal world when I came back from Yangon.
5. Michael W. Charney, A History of Modern Burma, (2009), p. 46.
6. During my field visit to Chittagon-Ramu-Cox's bazaar area I have seen quite

a number of Rakhine-Myanmar monasteries where manuscripts are carefully kept, as I have indicated in my works of 2010 and 2012. My field visit to Khamti villages of Namsai-Chongkham area of Arunachal Pradesh also gave me the impression that a large number of religious (Buddhist) scriptures in form of palm leave manuscripts etc are in private hands or stored in the monasteries that I have visited.

7. There is a detailed discussion of the Myanmar cultural model in my article 'Migration Acculturation and integration of Myanmar Tribes in India: Khamtis and Singphos of Arunachal Pradesh', 2005.
8. S. Bhattacharya (2013), p. 311 and Taw Sein Ko, 1920, p. 416.
9. Aung Thaw (1978); Pamela Gutman, 2001.
10. Swapna Bhattacharya, 'Religion and Colonial Politics: Assam, Myanmar and Buddhism' Jayanta Kumar Ray and Rakhee Bhattacharya (eds) *Development Dynamics in North East India* (MAKAIAS Publication) Delhi: Anghat Publishing House, 2008.
11. K.S. Singh, p. 133.
12. Spiro, p. 166.
13. S. Bhattacharya (1994 & 1997).
14. Various official agreements and MOUs have been signed by the two sides. The visit of India's former President Dr. A.P.J. Abdul Kalam to Myanmar in 2006 opened a new period of academic cooperation. A large number of Myanmar monks are now studying Pali, Buddhism, Sanskrit in various universities like Magadha, Nava Nalanda, Nagpur, Calcutta. Also significant is the visit of former Indian Prime Minister Dr. Manmohan Singh to Myanmar in 2012 following which a series of official agreements were signed. Eastern India especially West Bengal featured well in these tie-ups. The University of Dagon and University of Calcutta signed an MOU for collaboration in various academic fields.
15. B. Banerjee (2005), p. 270.
16. Barasambodhi Thera (2008), p. 23.
17. Ven. Nyanissara Mahathera (2009).
18. Aung Thaw, Gordon Luce, Niharranjan Roy, Pamela Gutman, Donald Stadtner.
19. Myint Aung, 2012.
20. The most interesting chapter is 'The Cult of Fertility and Myanmar's Ponmagyi'. I have discussed parallel experiences in the lives of Bengali and Myanmar people in my article 'Experiencing the Continuity in Art, Culture & Life in Bengal and Myanmar'.
21. Bhikkhu Kondinya (1986).
22. B. Tripathy and S. Dutta, p. 235.

## REFERENCES

Aung Thaw (1978), *Historical Sites in Burma*. Ministry of Union Culture, Govt. of the Union of Burma.

Aung, Htin (1962), *Folk Elements in Burmese Buddhism*. London: Oxford University Press.

Ahir, D.C. (2003), *Buddhist Sites and Shrines in India: History, Art and Architecture*. N.Delhi: Sri Satguru Publications.

Bagchi, Prabodh Chandra (1981), *India and China: A Thousand years of Cultural Relations*. Calcutta: Saraswat Library.

Banerjee, Biswanath (2004), 'Buddhism and Syncretism', *Journal of the Asiatic Society*, Kolkata, Vol.46, pp. 1-10.

Banerjee, Biswanath (2005), 'Kalacakra School' in Banerjee, Biswanth & Chaudhury, Sukomal (eds.) *Buddha and Buddhism*. Kolkata: Asiatic Society, pp. 266-275.

Barua, Brahmanda Pratap (2010), *Directory of Theravada Buddhist Temples in Eastern India,* Kolkata: All India Federation of Bengali Buddhists.

Bauddhacarya Shanti Swaroop Baudh (2012), *Sarnath: The Great Holy Place of Buddhists,* N. Delhi: Samyak Prakashan (translated by Moses Michael).

Bechert, Heinz, 'Renaissance of Buddhism in Indonesia', *Journal of the department of Pali*, Vol. 1, University of Calcutta, pp. 24-30.

Bechert, Heinz (1967), *Buddhism Staat und Gesellschaft in den Laendern des Theravada* Buddhism, Vols. 2 & 3, Wiesbaden: otto Harassowitz.

Bechert, Heinz (1996), 'To be a Burmese is to be a Buddhist: Buddhism in Burma' in H. Bechert & Richard Gombrich (eds.) *The world of Buddhism*. London: Thames and Hudsons

Bhattacharya, Swapna (1994), 'The Ari Cult of Myanmar'. *Tradition and Modernity in Myanmar,* edited by U. Gaertner and J. Lorenz, Southeast Asia Institute, Humboldt University, Berlin. Vol. 3/2, 1994, pp. 251-271. Special issue of the journal *Berliner Asien Afrika Studien.*

Bhattacharya, Swapna (1997), 'Some Observations on Mahayana—Tantric Beliefs in Ancient Myanmar', *Journal of the Department of Indian History and Culture*, Calcutta University, Vol. 20, pp. 52-67.

Bhattacharya, Swapna (2005), 'Migration Acculturation and Integration of Myanmar Tribes in India: Khamtis and Singphos of Arunachal'. Delhi: Anamika Publishers & Distributors, Published for Maulana Abul Kalam Azad Institute of Asian Studies, Kolkata, pp.145-187.

Bhattacharya, Swapna (2005), 'History of Buddhism in Myanmar: Interpretation from Indian Perspective', *Journal of the Asiatic Society*, Vol. XLVII, No.4 Kolkata: pp. 65-81.

Bhattacharya, Swapna (2005), 'From Mahabodhi Movement of the late 19th century (1891) to Neo-Buddhist Revival (1956) in Post Colonial India', in: *Myanmar Historical Commission Conference Proceedings* Pt. II. (12-14 January 2005), Yangon: Golden Jubilee Publication Committee, Myanmar Historical Commission, Ministry of Education, Union of Myanmar, pp. 339-359.

Bhattacharya, Swapna (2007), *India-Myanmar relations 1886-1948*, Kolkata: K.P. Bagchi & Co.

Bhattacharya, Swapna (2008), 'Religion and Colonial Politics: Assam, Myanmar and Buddhism' in Jayanta Kumar Ray and Rakhi Bhattacharys (eds.) *Development Dynamics in North East India.* Delhi: Anshah Publishing House, 309-329 (Maulana Abul kalam Azad Institute of Asian Studies, Kolkata).

Bhattacharya, Swapna (2010), *India and Myanmar: People, Pilgrimage, Histories and the Present*, Occasional paper: Centre for South & Southeast Asian Studies. University of Calcutta.

Bhattacharya, Swapna (2011), 'Contribution of Kripasaran Mahasthavir in the World of Buddhist Reform and Buddhist scholarship of the 19th century; India and beyond', *Jagajjyoti 2555 Buddha Jayanti* Volume. (ed.) Hemendu Bikash Chowdhuy, Kolkata: Bauddha Dharamnkur Sabha (Bengal Buddhist association), 88-93.

Bhattacharya, Swapna (2012), 'Situating Pilgrimage: Evaluating the Role of Myanmar Monasteries in South Asia' (ed.) Suchandana, Chatterjee, Anita Sengupta, & Susmita Bhattacharya, *Buddhism in Asia: Traditions and Imageries*. Delhi: Shipra publications.

In the Publication series of Maulana Abul Kalam Azad Institute of Asian Studies, pp. 92-135.

Bhattacharya, Swapna (2013), 'Experiencing the Continuity in Art, Culture & life in Bengal and Myanmar', *Journal of Bengal Art*, Vol. 18, (ed.) Professor Enamul Haque, Dhaka: The International Centre for study of Bengal Art, pp. 305-316.

Bhattacharya, Swapna (2014), 'Gurudev Rabindranath Tagore in the minds of the Myanmar people' in Mamata Desai, Manis Kumar Rajha & Chitra Ghosh (eds.) *Rabindranath Tagore: A many Splendoured Personality*, Kolkata: K.P. Bagchi & Co. pp. 118-141 (Netaji Institute of Asian Studies, Kolkata).

Bhattacharya, Swapna (In Press), 'The University of Calcutta and Myanmar: Urgent Need for revisiting the Golden Era', Paper presented at the Annual Conference of Myanmar Academy of Arts and Sciences 2012 (24-27 October, 2012), held at Yangon University.

Bhikkhu, Kondinya (1982), *Monastic Buddhism among Khamtis of Arunachal*, N. Delhi, National Publishing House.

Charney, Michael W. (2006), *Powerful Learning: Buddhist Literati and the Throne in Burma's Last Dynasty, 1752-1885*. Ann Abor, Centre for South & Southeast Asian Studies, The University of Michigan.

Duroiselle, Ch. (1990), 'The ari Cult and Tantric Buddhism', In *Annual Report of Archaeological Survey of India* 1915-1916, Delhi, 79-93 (Reprint).

Dutta Choudhuy (1978), *Gazetteer of India, Arunachal Pradesh, Lohit* District. Shillong: published by Shri M.P Hazarika. Director of Information & Public Relations, Govt. of Arunachal Pradesh.

Gogoi, Lila (1971), The *Tai Khamtis of Northeast India*, N. Delhi, Omsons Publications.

Guha, Devaprosad (1961-62), 'Buddhism and Burma,' in: *Indo-Asian Culture*, Vol. 10 (1961-62), 329-335 (as found in Heinz Bechert's *Buddhism, Staat und Gesellschaft in* den *Laendern des Theravada Budhism*, Vol. 3, Wiesbaden, Otto Harrassowitz, p. 135.

Gupta, Rita (2009), 'Contribution of Foreign Buddhist Monasteries in propagation of Buddhism' in Mukherjee, Ramaranjan (editor-in-chief) & Bhattacharya, Buddhadeva (editor), *Dimensions of Buddhism and Jainism*. Kolkata: Sanskrit Book Depot, Vol. I, pp. 374-383. Professor Suniti Kumar Pathak Felicitation Volume.

Gutman. Pamela (2001), *Burma's Lost Kingdom*: *Splendours of Arakan*, Bangkok: Orchid Press (Photography by Zaw Min Yu).

U Khin Maung Nyunt (Dr). (2002), *An Anthology of Conference papers. Prof. Dr. Khin Maung Nyunt*, Dept. of Archaeology, University of Yangon.

Khin Maung Nyunt (Dr), 'Indo-Myanmar Cultural Relations: past, Present and future' in Arindam Mukherjee (ed.) *Indo-Myanmar Relations: New Horizon,* Proceedings volume of an international Seminar orgnised by Institute of Social and Cultural Studies, India at the national Library, Kolkata February 8-9, 2014, pp. 9-15.

Ko, Taw Sein (1920), *Burmese Sketches*, Vol. II, Rangoon, British Burma Press.

Luce. Gordon (1969), *Old Burma Early Pagan*, Vol. I, New York, JJ Augstin Publisher Locust Valley.

Myint Aung, *Revealing Myanmar's Past: An Anthology of Archaeological Articles*, Yangon: Tun Foundation Bank Literary Committee (Tun Foundation Award), 2012.

Manguin, Pierre-Yves Mani, A. and Wade, Geoff (eds.) (2011), *Early Interactions between South and Southeast Asia: Reflections on Cross-Cultural Exchange*, Singapore: Institute of Southeast Asian Studies & India: Monohar.

Nyanissara Mahathera (2009), 'Buddhism in Myanmar', *Jagajjyoti (1908-2008). Centenary Volume,* Kolkata: Bauddha Dharmankur Sabha' (ed.) Chowdhury, Hemendu Bikash, pp. 206-210.

Ray, Niharranjan (2001), *Brahmanical Gods in Burma*, Bangkok: Orchid Press (first pub. 1932).

Ray, Niharranjan (2002), *Sanskrit Buddhism in Burma*, Bangkok: Orchid Press (first pub 1936).

Sarkar, Jayanta (1987), *Society, Culture and Ecological Adaptation among three tribes of Arunachal Pradesh*, Calcutta, Anthropological Survey of India, Ministry of Human Resource Development.

Sarkisyanz, Emanuel (1965), *The Buddhist Background of the Burmese Revolution*, The Hague: Martinus Nijhoff.

Sayagyi U Ba Khin, 'The Essentials of Buddha Dhamma in Practice' in *Buddha and Buddhism* (ed.) Biswanath Banerjee & Sukomal Chaudhuri, The Asiatic Society, Kolkata, 276-283.

Spiro, Melford E. (1982), *Buddhism and Society: A Great Tradition and its Burmese Vicissitudes,* Berkeley, University of California Press,

Sengupta, Sukumar, 'A History of the Pali Studies in the University of Calcutta (1880-1983)' in Haldar (De), Manikuntala (ed.) *Centenary Volume of the Department of Pali*, Kolkata, University of Calcutta, 2010, pp.41-86.

Singh, K.S. (ed). (1995), *People of India (Arunachal Pradesh)*, Vol. XVV, Kolkata: *Anthropological Survey of India.*

Stadtner, Donald. M. (2011), *Sacred Sites of Burma: Myth and Folklore in an Evolving Spiritual Realm.* Bangkok: River Books.

Strachan, Paul (1988), *Pagan: Art and Architecture of Old Burma.* Whiting Bay, Arran: Kiscadale.

Daw Than Tin. 'Kushinagar ka Adhunik Itihas' in Ven. Agga Maha Pandita Bhadanta Gyaneshwar (Chief editor) (2007), *Nibban Bodhi*, Vol. 1, Kushinagar: Kushinagar bhikkhu Sangh, p. 1.

U Tin Htway (1987), 'A Preliminary Note on the Vinayadharas of Pagan period in Burma', in: Diehl-Eli, Barbara, Servugian, Emanuel & Htway Tin (eds.) *Festschrift fuer Professor Manuel Sarkisyanz*, Frankfurt: Peter Lang, pp. 411-458.

Tripathy, B. (Dr) & Dutta, S. (Prof.) (2008), *Religious History of Arunachal Pradesh,* New Delhi: Gyan Publishing House.

Ven. Agga Maha Pandita Bhadanta Gyaneshwar (Chief editor) (2007), *Nibban Bodhi.* Vol. 1, Kushinagar: Kushinagar Bhikkhu Sangh.

Ven. Dr. Varasambodhi Thera (2008), 'Satabdir Alokita Manishi Sangharaja Dr. Rastrapala Mahathera' in idem (ed.) *Dhammadhaja: Sangharaja & 79th Birthday Celebration Volume of Ven. Dr. Rastrapala Mahathera.* Bodhgaya: International Meditation Centre, pp. 7-32.

**Acknowledgements:** First and foremost I would like to pay respect and express my deep sense of gratitude to all the Sayadaws (monks) and my teachers, whom I have mentioned in my present writing. They have enriched my soul and helped me to understand the core teachings of the Buddha. I am indebtedness to Dr. Sreeradha Dutta, Director, MAKAIAS for inviting me to this very important workshop-cum-seminar on Buddhism. I am thankful to Dr. Suchandana Chatterjee, Dr. Susmita Bhattacharya and Dr. Mrinal Chakma, three of my former colleagues from MAKAIAS, for their keen interest in my work. I shall be failing in my duty if I don't acknowledge the constant inspiration that I have been receiving over the years from Professor Jayanta Kumar Ray, currently Maulana Azad Fellow and formerly Chairman, MAKAIAS. To Professor Tansen Sen, who chaired the session in which this paper was presented I remain grateful too. To Hon'ble Minister Chowna Mein and Mrs. Sati Nang Mein (Hon'ble Member of Arunachal Pradesh Assembly) I remain ever so grateful for the invitation to witness the Golden Pagoda Dedication Ceremony and visits to several Buddhist (Myanmar style) monasteries in Namsai-Chongkham area of Arunachal Pradesh. The Consul General of Myanmar of the Republic of the Union of Myanmar in Kolkata U Kyaw Swe Tint helped me in understanding the true nature of Myanmar Buddhism through discussion, as and when needed. Such and other help I received from all his predecessors. In my journey for the Truth my husband, Dr. Debaprosad Chakraborti (former Head of the Department, Zoology, Presidency College, Kolkata) covered with me hundreds of kilometre, stretching from Lumbini to Namsai-Chongkham.. The excellent photos that I have in my possession and I have shown only a tiny part of them, in my presentation, could be made only due to his help. I thank him for all his help and inspiration.

**Dedication:** I dedicate this essay to my very respected teacher, Saya U Tin Htway, former Lecturer in Myanmar Language and Literature, South Asia Institute (Suedasien Institut) of Heidelberg University. Saya taught me not only Myanmar language, but also made me aware to be more attentive to the importance of Pali. I also tried to learn from his life how to develop equanimity, *Upekkha* through *Metta*, loving kindness.

# 3

# ENGAGED BUDDHISM: LOCATING SPACE IN THE ASIAN CONTEXT

*Anand Singh*

The Copernicus-Newton era integrated human progress with scientific inventions. This human progress has been identified with incorrigible consumerism, unbridled greed and insane desire to conquer the nature. It started jeopardising the equilibrium of the Universe, which consequently resulted in acid rain, green house effect, droughts and floods. In the twentieth century, the devastating effects of such anthropocentricism could be felt in every walk of human life that emanated some new approaches and dimensions to examine the academic and theological interpretations of human relations with nature and consequent ecological degeneration. The scholars, monks, and lay followers engaging themselves in Buddhology also started taking keen interest to investigate and apply Buddhist doctrines for environmental concerns. It created widespread movements in the whole of Southeast Asia, popularly known as 'Engaged Buddhist Movements'. However, the methodology and technique of each of such nation are different from each other and have evolved according to the local requirements and traditions.

The Engaged Buddhists prefer and popularise their traditions to get some positive response for environmentalism. Some of them are even known as 'ecology monks', who engage themselves to focus their work on deforestation and adopt some rituals and teachings in order to help local population to protect forests. They took strong views against the government and contractors, especially in Thailand, for the short-sighted policy of forest farming. They inculcate eco-friendly policies of agriculture and teach the peasants about harmful consequences of deforestation. The farming community is generally ignorant about relationship between cutting of trees and hardship they suffer from land erosion, flood, aridity etc. The 'ecology monks' of Thailand perform Buddhist rituals that give a religious meaning to a tree, and adopt traditional practices in which a laity donates tree saplings to the monasteries. These tree saplings are planted around the monasteries under the reforestation programme.

The seed of engaged Buddhism was blossomed by Joanna Macy and Deane Curtin, who used Buddhist texts and traditions to counter the anthropocentric worldview. Joanna Macy says that the conventional notion of the self should be ecological self or the eco-self, co-extensive with other beings and the life of our planet. She calls it 'the greening of the self' and further argues that the ecological self is arising:

> 'because of three converging developments. First, the conventional small self, or ego-self is being impinged upon by the psychological and spiritual effects we are suffering from facing the dangers of mass annihilation. The second thing working to dismantle the ego-self is a way of seeing that has arisen out of science itself. It is called the systems view, cybernetics, or a new paradigm science. From this perspective, life is seen as dynamically composed of self-organizing systems, patterns that are sustained in and by their relationships. The third force is the resurgence in our time of non dualistic spiritualities. Here I am speaking from my experience with Buddhism.'[1]

Macy admits that 'the abstraction of a separate 'I' is a epistemological fallacy of Western civilization' as proved by scientific inquiry, and cites:

> 'Contemporary science and system science in particular, goes farther in challenging old assumptions about a distinct, separate, continuous self, by showing that there is no logical or scientific basis for construing one part of experienced world as "me" and the rest as "other". That is so because as open, self-organizing systems, our breathing, acting and thinking arise in interaction with our shared world through the currents of matter, energy and information that move through us and sustain us. In the web of relationships that sustain these activities there is no clear line demarcating separate continuous self.'[2]

To popularise their idea John Seed and Joanna Macy developed the 'Council of All Beings" as a way to introduce people to deep ecology. The Council facilitates rituals for expressing grief over the loss of many species and impart lessons to people to speak for other beings with compassion.[3] H.H. Dalai Lama, Thich Nhat Hanh, Lo Zen Rosha, John Daido Loori and Robert Aitkin take deep ecology route to popularise environmentalism.[4] H.H. Dalai Lama says that modern science and technology, though capable of creating infinite material comfort, cannot replace the age old spiritual and humanitarian values that have largely shaped the world civilisation. His speeches and action have created gradual and sustained awareness for environmentalism. He gives the example of how the survival of life on earth is threatened by human activities, which lack commitment to humanitarian values. Destruction of nature and natural resources may be because of ignorance, greed or lack of respect for earth's living beings. Many of the earth's habitats, animals, plants, insects and micro-organism became extinct or endangered. It is the responsibility of human-beings to save them.[5]

Seth Devere Clippard in his essay *The Lorax Wears Saffron: Towards a Buddhist Environmentalism* locates two different strategies applied by the protagonists of Buddhist environmentalists in Thailand. One being textual and other applied.[6] In the 1980s, the

Thai environmental activist Ajahan Pongsak Techathamamoo started engaging the monks in rural areas to restore the forest surroundings after decades of ill-conceived deforestation. Thus, Engaged Buddhism in Thailand started ordination of trees, which were wrapped in saffron robes to signify their status as a monk. The first tree ordination was performed in 1988 by Phrakhru Manas Natheepitak, the abbot of Wat Bodharma in northern Thailand, in response to the drought caused by excessive logging that adversely affected the rivers and indigenous eco-system. Manas did not offer solution through traditional Buddhist teaching like *paticcasamuppada* but intended that the tree wrapped in robe would not be harmed by the people because of its religious sanctity. The ordained tree is at par with a monk and the people will not be willing to lose their merit by harming it. His effort was fruitful and the Thai government imposed ban on logging.[7]

Susan Darlington has explained extensively about 'ecology monks' who actively engage in conservation activities and respond to the sufferings that are caused by environmental degradation. The preference of these monks is actions to preserve the resources of vanishing forests, water sources and wildlife in order to mitigate the negative consequences of their disappearance on the people's lives. She studied the life of a well known 'ecology monk' Pharakhru Pitak Nanthakhun, who had adopted the practice of tree ordination but applied it in different manner by citing the examples of basic tenets of the Buddha such as *paticcasamuppada* that highlights a close relationship of mankind with forest.[8]

Donald K. Swearer examined the activities of two monks who were related to *bodhirukkha* movement in Thailand. Buddhadasa's ecological view identifies *dhamma* with nature and Phrayudha focuses on the life of the Buddha and traditional *sangha* as an exemplification of the Buddhist attitude towards nature.[9] Sulak Sivaraksa encouraged the environmentalism founded on fundamental

Buddhist principles. The aim of such movements is to initiate the Buddhist economics with pragmatic programmes which can regenerate depleting forests. The Thai monk Pongsak Tejadhamma started ordination of trees in Chiang Mai province of Thailand along with a number of monks, and ordination was done according to strict *Vinaya* rules.[10] The monks are fully aware that the ordination is only symbolic because *patimokkha* rules allow to ordinate only human beings. They were criticised from within and outside the *sangha* saying that such ordination was not conducive to Buddhist tenets.[11] Some monastic people objected to the tree ordination and expelled the monks who supported it because *pabajja* could be given only to humans. It was considered inappropriate because the symbolic ritual was performed to make people aware about forest conservation, and the monks were doing it symbolically without claiming it as full ordination.[12] Clippard says that the 'linguistic analogy' was used by the 'ecology monks' for practical purpose.

> 'The monk is the signifier, the tree is the signified, and the ordination is the signification. On the one hand, the meaning of the ordination should go after (the statement) roughly the same regardless of the signified. On the other hand, the statement in which the tree is the signified produces radically different effect on the listener for whom the signification (ordination) is meaningful. The signified, having been modified by the signification, challenges the listener to adjust his/her relationship to the signified in light of the new semantic values attached to the signified. That is, the members of the Buddhist community are challenged to understand what an ordained tree means....'[13]

Whatever debate has been going on concerning the 'ecology monks' in Thailand, it not only created awareness about environmentalism but provided the methods and tools to implement it, and it has been best exemplified by Phrakhru Manas in *Dharma Gaia.*

> 'If a tree is wrapped in saffron robes, no one would dare cut it down. So I thought that perhaps this idea could be used to discourage logging,

and I began performing ceremonies on trees in the forest near the temple. I called the ritual an 'ordination' to give it more weight. The term 'tree ordination' sounds weird to Thai people since an ordination is a ritual applied only to men. This weirdness has helped spread the news by word of mouth.'[14]

In 1958, A.T. Ariyaratne with a small band of young followers started the 'engaged movement' *Sarvodaya* in Sri Lanka and their self-help groups are active in 4000 towns and villages. These groups are involved in health, sanitation, education, agriculture and rural economy. The vision of the movement is sustainable development without eroding the socio-cultural fabric of the society. Ariyaratne is highly critical of the 'development model' adopted by both socialist and capitalist forms of governments, because, in his opinion, the development programmes would not be effective without cultural and spiritual values.[15] He says that nature is an important element and considered sacred among the people of Sri Lanka. He cites Buddhist *suttas* to argue that nothing in nature should be spoiled or wasted for wanton desires as it can upset the natural balance of life and eco-system. Destroying the natural resources is not only a physical pollution but also has degenerating effect on eco-system. The philosophy of *Sarvodaya* is based on compassionate action, altruistic joy, equanimity, as well as, pleasant speech and friendly treatment with people of different origin and ethnicity. The people are encouraged to come out and participate in a way of life and on a path of development founded on these ideals.[16] The *Sarvodaya* movement revitalized the rural life and folk culture of Sri Lanka not only by initiating the development projects but also by working as 'conflict resolution model' to mellow down the conflicts among various warring groups for progress and peace.

In the war ravaged society of Vietnam, Thich Nhat Hanh encouraged the Buddhist community to practice harmony and awareness in the Vietnamese society. He offered meditation retreats for environmentalists, which opened the possibilities for men and women to sit and practice meditation. He initiated the 'engaged mission' in two ways. Firstly, by adopting psychological approach with the help of *Abhidhamma* to solve the problems of internal strife and restore peace by reliving the suffering from inside. Secondly, through the regulations of the Buddhist approach to harmony and peace as well as the Buddhist spirit of reverence of life.[17] He recommends:

> 'Our ecology should be a deep ecology—not only deep, but universal. There is pollution in our consciousness.'[18]

Hanh suggests coping mechanism by recitation of *gathas*. When one's mind concentrate on *gathas*, it becomes more aware about an action and when the *gatha* ends, the action continues with much awareness and promptness. The *gathas* of Hanh reminds us of our responsibility towards environmentalism.

> *Water flows from high in the mountains*
> *Water runs deep in the Earth.*
> *Miraculously, water comes to us,*
> *and sustains all life.*[19]

W.S. Yokoyama in his essay *Circling the Mountain* studies the Engaged Buddhist tradition in Japan. He argues that the Buddhist meditation can be instrumental for preservation and development of environment-friendly society, but rejects the idea of meditation as a mindless mystical trance. The meditation technique develops a state of calm in which mental forces and correct awareness play substantial role in dissolving dualistic thought and reducing mental dullness and anxiety. To substantiate his points he takes three examples of the Buddhist life of Japan: (i) a Tendai Monastery, (ii) a Zen Temple and (iii) a Shin home.[20] The Tendai Monastery is ritualistic in nature and situated on Mount Hiei where pilgrims come for thousand-day pilgrimage. During such event he/she walks daily despite hostile winter or hot humid climate to reach at a point where one enters in a realm of 'oneness with nature'. Yokoyama accepts that there are only few who will go for such arduous journey but there can be something suggestive about the pilgrim's experience of 'becoming with nature'. With growing urbanization and industrialization of Japanese society the modern life has become more complex and devoid of nature. The thousand day's journey reverses such trends and as the practice deepens one enters into communion with the benign beauty of the Universe, its forests, rocks and flowers. It is not only aesthetic but also leads to close acquaintance with nature, beyond the world of delusion created by human mind.[21]

Yokoyama cites his second example from the gathering of lay followers on every Sunday morning in a Zen temple. The lay people not only listen to religious discourses but discuss the general problems of the Japanese society. The environmental concern is a major concern for them. In this context, the remark of a monk is worth mentioning here:

> 'If this trend continues what will happen to us? Are we buy our air in bottles, just as we buy bottled water'.[22]

At present, the monks of the Zen temple are no longer associated to Samurais and feudal elite classes but represent all section of the society. The methodology used by Zen masters, to awaken their disciples, such as *koan* (puzzle) to test the intellectual depth of students, makes them aware of the current environmentalism.

Yokoyama's third example is from a Shin temple family which has strong feeling for its religion and belongs to the agricultural community of Japan. Their Buddha is a dynamic force working for their salvation and a force dynamically engaged in helping others. The Shin emphasises on individual and emboldens us to consider our actions in life, because in the environmentally compromised world human action is important to bear in mind, not just living in an environmentally protective life but also in our personal relations with others.[23] Thus, engaged Buddhism despite some controversies is playing a great role in the formation of environmental ethics.

## NOTES

1. Macy, Joanna, "The Greening of the Self", in Badiner, Allan Hunt (ed.), *Dharma Gaia: A Harvest of Essays in Buddhism and Ecology,* California: Parallax Press, 1990, pp. 53, 55.
2. *Ibid.* p. 58.
3. Devall, Bill, "Deep Ecology and Political Activism", in Kaza, Stephanie and Kenneth Kraft (eds.), *Dharma Rain: Sources of Buddhist Environmentalism,* Boston: Shambhala, 2000, p. 390.
4. Clippard, Seth Devere, "The Lorex Wears Saffron: Towards a Buddhist Environmentalism", *Journal of Buddhist Ethics,* Vol. 18, 2011, p. 214.
5. Dalai Lama XIV, *Tree of Life: Buddhism and Protection of Nature,* Buddhist Perception of Nature, 1987, pp. 95-98.
6. Clippard, Seth Devere, *op. cit.,* p. 212,
7. Darlington, Susan M., "The Good Buddha and the Fierce Spirits: Protecting the Northern Thai Forest", *Contemporary Buddhism: An Interdisciplinary Journal,* Volume 8, Issue 2, 2007, Special Issue: Buddhism and the Environment, pp. 169-185.
8. Darlington, Susan M., *The Ordination of a Tree,* Albany: SANY (State University of New York) Press, 2013, pp. 2-8.
   (Phrakhru Pitak Nanthakun has been most successful in applying the ordination ritual in his native province Nan in northern Thailand. He combined the tree ordination with *phaa paa,* a traditional Buddhist ceremony in which lay followers offer money and goods to monks. He received the offerings of tree seedlings rather than funds or goods. In 1991 he did his first tree ordination and tree seedling in Kew Muang in which the entire forest was sanctified with Buddhist rituals - Udomittipong, Pipob, "Thailand's Ecology Monks", in Kaza, Stephanie and Kenneth Kraft, (eds.) *Dharma Rain: Sources of Buddhist Environmentalism,* Boston: Shambhala, 2000, pp. 196-197).
9. Swearer, Donald K., "The Hermeneutics of Buddhist Ecology in Contemporary Thailand: Buddhadasa and Dhammapitaka", in Mary Evelyn Tucker and Duncan Ryuken Williams (eds.), *Buddhism and Ecology: The Interconnection of Dharma and Deeds,* Cambridge, MA: Harvard University Press, pp. 21-44. (Buddhadasa Bhikshu condemned Thai government's attempt to prohibit the teaching *of santutthi.)*
10. Harris, Ian, "Buddhism and Ecology", in Damien Keown (ed.), *Contemporary Buddhist Ethics,* Richmund, Surrey: Curzon Press, 2000, p. 118.
11. Darlington, Susan M., "The Good Buddha and the Fierce Spirits: Protecting the Northern Thai Forest", *op. cit.*, pp. 170,178
12. Darlington, Susan M., *The Ordination of a Tree, op. cit.*, p. 200.

13. Clippard, Seth Devere, *op. cit.,* pp. 228-229.
14. Udomittipong, Pipob, "Thailand's Ecology Monks", in Kaza, Stephanie and Kenneth Kraft, (eds.) *Dharma Rain: Sources of Buddhist Environmentalism,* Boston: Shambhala, 2000, p. 193.
15. Ariyaratne, A.T. and Joanna Macy, "The Island of Temple and Tank", in Batchelor, Martine and Brown Kerry (eds.), *Buddhism and Ecology*, New Delhi: MLBD, 1994, pp. 78-79.
16. *Ibid.*, p. 82.
17. Batchelor, Martin, "Look Deep and Smile: The Thoughts and Experiences of a Vietnamese Monk", in Batchelor, Martine and Brown Kerry (eds.), *Buddhism and Ecology,* New Delhi: MLBD, 1994, p. 101.
18. Thich Nhat Hant, *Present Moment, Wonderful Moment,* Berkeley, California: Parallax Press, 1990, p. 102.
19. *Ibid.*, p. 105.
20. Yokoyama, W.S., "Circling the Mountain: Observations on the Japanese way of life", in Batchelor, Martine and Brown Kerry (eds.), *Buddhism and Ecology*, New Delhi: MLBD, 1994, pp. 55-56.
21. *Ibid.*, pp. 59-60.
22. *Ibid.*, p. 60.
23. *Ibid.*, p. 64.

## REFERENCES

Ariyaratne, A.T. and Joanna Macy, "The Island of Temple and Tank", in Batchelor, Martine and Brown Kerry (eds.), *Buddhism and Ecology*, New Delhi: MLBD, 1994.

Badiner, Allan Hunt (ed.), *Dharma Gaia: A Harvest of Essays in Buddhism and Ecology*, California: Parallax Press, 1990.

Brown, Kerry, "In the Water There was a Fish and the Fields were Full of Rice", in Batchelor, Martine and Brown Kerry (eds.), *Buddhism and Ecology*, New Delhi: MLBD, 1994.

Batchelor, Martine and Brown Kerry (eds.), *Buddhism and Ecology*, New Delhi: MLBD, 1994.

Batchelor, Martin, "Look Deep and Smile: The Thoughts and Experiences of a Vietnamese Monk", in Batchelor, Martine and Brown Kerry (eds.), *Buddhism and Ecology*, New Delhi: MLBD, 1994.

Clippard, Seth Devere, "The Lorex Wears Saffron: Towards a Buddhist Environmentalism", *Journal of Buddhist Ethics*, Vol. 18, 2011.

Darlington, Susan M., "Tree Ordination in Thailand", in Kaza, Stephanie and

Kenneth Kraft. (eds.) *Dharma Rain: Sources of Buddhist Environmentalism*, Boston: Shambhala, 2000.

Devall, Bill, "Deep Ecology and Political Activism", in Kaza, Stephanie and Kenneth Kraft (eds.), *Dharma Rain: Sources of Buddhist Environmentalism*, Boston: Shambhala, 2000.

Harris, Ian, "Buddhism and Ecology", in Damien Keown (ed.), *Contemporary Buddhist Ethics*, Richmond, Surrey: Curzon Press, 2000.

Kaza, Stephanie and Kenneth Kraft (eds.), *Dharma Rain: Sources of Buddhist Environmentalism*, Boston: Shambhala, 2000.

Leopold, Aldo, "The Land Ethics", in Hugh La Follette (ed.) *Ethics in Practice: An Anthology*, Oxford: Blackwell, 1997.

Leopold, Aldo, *A Sand County Almanac*, Oxford University Press: Oxford, 1997.

Macy, Joanna, "The Greening of the Self", in Badiner, Allan Hunt, (ed.), Dharma Gaia, *A Harvest of Essays in Buddhism and Ecology*, California: Parallax Press, 1990.

Naess, Arne, "Deep Ecology", in Carolyn Merchant (ed.) *Ecology*, New Delhi: Rawat Publication, 1996.

Naess, Arne, "The Shallow and the Deep, Long-Range Ecology Movements: A Summary", *Inquiry: An Interdisciplinary Journal of Philosophy*, Vol.16, Issue 1-4, January 1973, pp. 95-100.

Parker, Kelly A, "Pragmatism and Environmental Thought", in Andrew Light and Eric Katz (eds.) *Environmental Pragmatism*, London: Routledge, 1996.

Singer, Peter, *Practical Ethics*, New Delhi: Cambridge University Press (Indian Edition), 2000.

Swearer, Donald K., "The Hermeneutics of Buddhist Ecology in Contemporary Thailand: Buddhadasa and Dhammapitaka", in Mary Evelyn Tucker and Duncan Ryuken Williams (eds.), *Buddhism and Ecology: The Interconnection of Dharma and Deeds*, Cambridge, Mass: Harvard University Press, 1997.

Udomittipong, Pipob, "Thailand's Ecology Monks", in Kaza, Stephanie and Kenneth Kraft (eds.), *Dharma Rain: Sources of Buddhist Environmentalism*, Boston: Shambhala, 2000.

Yokoyama, W.S., "Circling the Mountain: Observations on the Japanese way of life", in Batchelor, Martine and Kerry Brown, *Buddhism and Ecology*, New Delhi: MLBD, 1994.

# 4

# Tibetans in India: Socio-Cultural Adaptation

*Mamata Desai*

## Introduction

Religion has been one of the chief influences in modifying human attitudes and behaviors especially in the country like Tibet. In the past the religious influence in the most of the contemporary societies even in western countries was significantly high. With the advancement of science and technology in the western societies the religious beliefs and practices are on the decline. But to know Tibet it is very necessary to know about their religion. The Tibetan social and family structure, socio-cultural activities have been controlled by the religion i.e. Lamaistic Mahayana Buddhism. For centuries this religion had a vital role in day to day life of a Tibetan till 1950 when China strengthened its aggressive actions over Tibet. Before that the traditional Tibetan life was totally controlled by the Tibetan Buddhism. Today, after more than five decades in exile, the Tibetan population living in different parts of India has risen to about 1,22,078.

The map of Asia shows the mighty Himalayas as India's boundary in the north. Beyond the Himalayas lies the little known territory of Tibet, which is barren and dry, the homeland of the Tibetan people. Their religion is Lamaistic Buddhism, in which His Holiness The Dalai Lama is believed to be a reincarnation of the Buddha. The Buddhist Tibetans did not permit anyone except the Chinese, to enter the capital Lhasa, who prevented any trade between India and Tibet. In 1904 the Government of India was succeeded in sending a mission to Lhasa to establish trade relation, directly with Tibet. In 1910 Chinese invaded Tibet when British Government extended their protection, and Dalai Lama sought refuge in India. He returned to Tibet in 1913, and established its reign at Lhasa. However, as a landlocked territory, Tibet had to depend on China to certain extent for economic as well as social reasons. The Chinese and the Tibetan Government assigned at an agreement consisting of 17 points in the year 1951. The existing political system was not to be altered and the regional autonomy was to be enjoyed by the Tibet, under the agreement with the central peoples Government of China. But the agreement was repudiated and China became aggressor, when the Tibetan Head of the State, His Holiness the Dalai Lama and a large number of Tibetans were rather forced to flee from Tibet and sought refuge in India during 1959. Since 1959, along with the Dalai Lama a large number of Tibetans were settled in India and at other places of the world. They were rehabilitated in the different states of India where their education, culture and identity were preserved. At that time it was necessary to settle all the Tibetan refugees into cohesive homogenous society and setting up of schools for refugee children having their own curriculum. Several resettlement camps were opened by the Government of India to rehabilitate the Tibetans. Among them the following are important:

1. Bylakuppa in Karnataka,
2. Buxa in West Bengal,
3. Kalimpong in West Bengal,

4. Darjeeling in West Bengal,
5. Changlang in Arunachal Pradesh,
6. Tezu in Arunachal Pradesh,
7. Gangtok in Sikkim,
8. Dehra Dun in Uttarakhand,
9. Chandragiri in Orissa,
10. Dharamsala in Himachal Pradesh.

Dalai Lama himself stays at Dharamsala along with a number of refugees. Since 1959 majority of the Tibetan refugees moved into India. This abrupt change from one kind of social milieu and ecological set-up to a strikingly different one was a very difficult experience for the Tibetans. Along with climatic change, their occupation, food habits etc. also changed. The Tibetans did manage to flee to India, but were left completely destitute, having no other support. The Tibetans fled their homeland and entered into Indian Territory, where they hoped, they would have security of social life and freedom of religion. In India the value and need of preserving the Tibetan religious-intellectual tradition and some religious institutions were established by the Central Tibetan Administration and highly intellectual lamas were appointed to undertake the job.

## The Central Tibetan Administration in Dharamsala

The Tibetans in India have been able to preserve religious traditions among the refugees. Almost all the respondents who were interviewed have expressed their views accordingly. Most of the rituals related to the birth, death and marriage, which were traditionally practiced in Tibet, are performed by the refugees in exile with some modifications in some of the camps depending upon the culture, behavior and attitude of the neighboring host population. They have also stated that they have selected India as their host country because of their socio cultural and religious relations with India from times immemorial. They feel more at home in India rather than any other country. At the same time as time passes they are concerned about the newly emerging socio-economic forces for which their second generation especially who are born and brought up in India are affected. They are more materialistic and are trying to achieve economic success in their individual life. But still they all perform almost all religious ceremonies with sincerity.

## The History of Migration and some Tibetan Camps in India

Tibet lies in the northern slopes of the Himalayas. It is by and large a plateau whose political centre had always been in Central Tibet. The 'People's Liberation Army' invaded Tibet on 20th October 1950. On March 17 1959 it was decided that the Dalai Lama should leave Lhasa immediately, as in their view his life was in danger as per the report in *The Statesman*, Calcutta, March 26, 1959. The revolt of 1959 was confined to Lhasa and the immediate environs, which was crushed easily by the Chinese Liberation Army. But following the revolt, China's political and military presence in Tibet increased. As a result, the Dalai Lama, along with a large number of Tibetan refugees entered en masse into India, Bhutan & Nepal. Within five months 12,369 Tibetan refugees had taken shelter in India. After his exile to India, the Dalai Lama had issued a statement from Tezpur in 1959, "I left Lhasa and Tibet and came to India of my free will and not under duress" (NCNA—Peking April, 1959). There are number of reasons why Tibetans fled to India from their homeland Tibet where they were living from times immemorial. Surveys in different camp areas suggest that most them escaped to India or elsewhere because of persecution. The most important reason behind their escape was the departure of His Holiness the Dalai Lama. Many people followed him to India while some took shelter in Nepal or Bhutan or in USA, UK, Canada etc.

After the Chinese occupation of Tibet in 1959, when the Tibetan refugees followed His Holiness the Dalai Lama in exile to India, they were rehabilitated in the different states of India where their education, culture and social identity were preserved. The Dalai Lama approached the then Prime Minister of India Pandit Jawaharlal Nehru for his social cooperation and financial assistance in the rehabilitation process of the refugees who accepted the request and instructed different state governments to act accordingly. Karnataka (then Mysore) was the first state to accept 3,000 Tibetan refugees and offered 1500 hectares of uninhabited jungle in Bylakuppa in 1960. Thereafter, in 1962 second and third rehabilitation centers were set up in Arunachal Pradesh. Initially they were allotted two and a half hectares of land for the construction of houses and for agriculture purposes. Today they are practising agro-Industrial economy mostly along their traditional handicrafts like carpet weaving, apron and incense making. Today, after more than four decades in exile, there are total of 1,22,078 number of Tibetan refugees living worldwide. Majority of them are settled in fifty two settlements located in South Asia, of which thirty five are in India, ten in Nepal and seven in Bhutan.

## Social Structure of Tibetan Refugees: Past and Present

Religion has always exerted great influence on Tibetan society, particularly the two different segments of Tibetan social set up i.e., the lay society and the monastic one. This duality of the Tibetan society should be examined historically, and also as on the basis of ecological adaptation system.

The lay society of Tibet (before 1951) was a very stratified one, which consisted of elitist society and classified persons. Apart from the noble or elites, rich farmers and merchants, small traders were included in this category. Next came where the people belonged to minor occupations like carpenters, tailors and masons, and then the smiths, tinkers and butchers. Apparently there was no middle class.

The noble men of Tibet attributed their descent to three sources: first, the family in which a Dalai Lama was recognized as the reincarnation received large estate from the government, property that was granted to them, and only because of the received grant, they became the nobles of the society. Thus the families of the Dalai Lamas were treated as nobles of the society. Secondly there were the families, who were recognized and rewarded by the government for their past services to the state.

Thirdly, the families who traced their ancestry to the early monarchs that had reigned in Tibet, prior to the rule of the Dalai Lamas. In addition, sometimes new noble families were emerged through matrimonial alliances between the nobility of neighboring countries and accordingly became the nobles of Tibetan society.

As a rule, nobles could marry within their own society. Both polygamy and polyandry were practiced by them. The main objective was to save the property from being divided. The nobles earned their livelihood from three principal sources. Firstly, each noble family was granted estates by the government. One or two members of a family served as officials of the government. To become a government official, a young noble had to be trained in the government's finance office. As the salaries of the officials were negligible, the main sources of income were the family estates, and the services rendered by the officials were granted as 'kral' or tax.

Secondly, the name of the family was derived from the name of the estate, rewarded by the government. The leading families performed both agricultural and pastoral duties. Many nobles practised several trades. Thirdly, the many of the nobles had rug or blanket factories or some other trades. But the main source of income was landed property.

After the nobles, mention should be made about the peasantry of Tibet, because five-sixths of the total population was engaged in agriculture. Due to long winter and hasty climate, cropping seasons were not longer enough. Again the implements and methods used by the peasants were very primitive and simple; as a result crop yield per acreage was very low.

The herdsmen also played an important role in the lay society, because in a land of mixed economy where both agriculture and live stock breeding were practiced, the importance of herdsmen could not be ignored. The most important domestic animals kept by the Tibetans were yaks and sheep. The herdsmen had to remain within well-defined territory and routes determined by the government. The boundaries of their region, shifted along with climatic variations during winter and summer. They lived practically on animals and animal products. The butter, they used to prepare from milk of sheep or yak, were sent to the government treasury as part of their revenue, and the district administration in turn sent a portion of the butter to the monasteries for burning lamps in the temples. Tibetan herdsmen followed the different sects of Buddhism like other people, and their social life were controlled by religion. It is evident from, that they also used to send their sons to the monasteries to make them monks. The overall Tibetan society was controlled by different religious segments. As a result priests played a very important role in Tibet's social life. They were engaged to perform religious rites for the families, to cure illness, to perform rites after birth and death. Even the medical treatments were performed by the priests. Thus the lay society was almost fully dependent on monastic society. So in order to understand the social and political structure of Tibet, the structure and organizational influences of the monastic society and monasteries should be examined. There were altogether 1,800 monasteries of different categories, belonging to the ruling Geluk-Pa sect and other sects. During seventeenth century, the number of monks who lived in these monasteries was about 1,00,000. The Dalai Lama held the highest position in the monastic set-up.

## Social and Economic Life of Tibetan Refugees—in Exile

When Tibetans first came into exile, most of them were starving or wounded, sick from the low altitude and overpowered by the cultural shock of coming into distant world, with the result, many died of disease or likewise symptoms. Gradually, they were rehabilitated in the newly created settlements in south and central India. Tibetans were trained in cultivating local Indian crops like maize, millet, rice and mustard and soon after, agriculture became the main source of livelihood. At the same time Tibetans have started selling winter garments especially sweaters in streets of towns and cities of India. Today sweater business has become dominant economic activity for Tibetans in India. Although agriculture is a major primary occupation of Tibetans especially for those living in agricultural based settlements in south India.

Table 1 suggests that out of total number of respondents 5.63 percent were attached somehow to the agricultural activities, 9.09 percent belong to upper class society (holding dignified positions), 23.63 percent represent monks etc. (somehow attached to the monastery), 20.72 percent actively engaged with the Central Tibetan Administration, and the remaining 10.9 percent belong to the trader community

**Table 1: The Tibetan Refugees and their Livelihood Pattern in Exile**

| *Sr. No.* | *Occupational Status* | *No. of Respondents* | *Percentage of Respondents* |
|---|---|---|---|
| 1 | Attached to Agriculture | 98 | 5.63 |
| 2 | Elite | 25 | 9.09 |
| 3 | Religious personnel (monks) | 65 | 23.65 |
| 4 | Tibetan Administration | 57 | 20.72 |
| 5 | Traders | 30 | 10.90 |
| | Total 275 100.00 | | |

*Source:* Field Survey.

Table 2 shows the occupational status of the respondents, as was found in Tibet. From the point of view of the Tibetans' traditional occupational pattern the sample may be said well represented, as it mostly covers the livelihood patterns of the Tibetan society in their original homeland i.e., Tibet.

**Table 2: Tibetan Refugees and their livelihood in Tibet**

| *Sr. No.* | *Occupational Status* | *No. of Respondents* | *Percentage* |
|---|---|---|---|
| 1 | Attached Agriculture | 90 | 32.74 |
| 2 | Elite | 25 | 9.09 |
| 3 | Religious personnel | 75 | 27.27 |
| 4 | Herders | 42 | 15.27 |
| 5 | Traders | 43 | 15.63 |
| | Total | 275 | 100.00 |

*Source:* Field Survey.

According to Table 3, the largest percentage share of income that is forty one percent comes from Tibetans doing trade and business which includes selling garments and doing petty business. The salaried employment, which includes services in the army, government and teaching, contributes twenty three percent of the household income, whereas agricultural and allied activities account for twenty six of the total workforce contributing a mere eight percent of the total household income. Apart from the primary sources of income, the Tibetan households also rely on subsidiary sources of income, which include income from sponsorships, government and foreign remittances. Many of the economically deprived households are either being looked after by the government or are supported by the sponsors from abroad.

**Table 3: Sources of Income of the Tibetan Refugees in Exile**

| *Economic Activities* | *%age share of income* | *%age share of workforce* |
|---|---|---|
| Agriculture & allied activities | 8.5 | 26.4 |
| Artisans and crafts | 4.2 | 5.7 |
| Hotels and restaurant | 3.3 | 1.9 |
| Organized trade or business | 30.7 | 16.2 |
| Professional job | 0.6 | 0.3 |
| Salaried employment | 23.0 | 20.1 |
| Small enterprises | 14.1 | 12.1 |
| Unorganized trade or business | 10.7 | 11.1 |
| Casual work | 4.8 | 6.2 |

*Source:* Field Survey.

In a study of social change, the hierarchical pattern of the traditional society is an important factor, which is discussed already. The strong emotional hierarchical system is glaring in the present set-up of the Tibetans in India. The old orthodox system is no longer feasible in the new ecological set-up. As a result, though the Tibetans are still trying to maintain their traditional protocol and cultures, it is practically impossible for them to retain or continue the same practices in India.

The process of change which has affected the Tibetans in India has been examined in the light of past social hierarchical system and stratified patterns. As such it is necessary to study at a glance the system of traditional hierarchical and stratified structure of the Tibetan society. The table given below will give an idea about it.

**Table 4: Hierarchical and Stratified Social Structure of the Tibetan Society**

In their Homeland

The Dalai Lama / The Panchen Lama

| | |
|---|---|
| The lay Society | The Monastic Society |
| ↓ | ↓ |
| The Nobles | La-Chi or University Board |
| ↓ | ↓ |
| Big Merchants and Landlords | Dra Tshong (the College) |
| ↓ | ↓ |
| Rich Traders, Peasantry and herdsmen | Ordinary Monks Khamtsten |
| ↓ | |
| Craftsmen, traders | |
| ↓ | |
| Beggars, Butchers | |

In the new situation, along with the changing mode of occupation the traditional hierarchical system has been broken. Services, business have emerged as two new and principal occupational divisions. Even in administrative establishment of Dalai Lama, various service institutions have emerged to cater to the newly educated generation. At the same time the proportion of agriculturists has not declined. Moreover, the fact is that the numbers of farmers are greater than that of the service holders because agricultural settlements are more in number than the administrative establishments. Table 7 will explain the changing mode of occupations.

## The Values of Family and Marriage: Past and Present

Family is the foundation of a larger social structure. To study social change of a particular human group it is necessary to examine the kinship and structure of the family, which is very complex and comprehensive. In this present work, only the major structural features of the traditional family will be studied in the light of the changes those were observed in the Tibetan refugee family in India in an entirely different ecological set-up.

The system of polygamy and polyandry were both practiced in Tibet. The system of polyandry helped to limit the birth rate, and thus kept the family small and the population level remained almost constant. It also had a good effect on maintaining the higher standard of living than neighboring countries. Despite inadequate resources, there was enough food for all. The type of polyandry which was practiced in Tibet was of fraternal-polyandry—(brothers sharing the same wife where marriage had been formally solemnized with the eldest brother).

It is evident that to Tibetans any form of marriage was acceptable, provided it would prevent fragmentation of landed property. Traditionally, marriages were arranged by the parents and abided by strict rules of endogamy and exogamy. The main objectives were to save family property from disintegration, to maintain the purity of the family stock and to retain class distinctions. All these had made the Tibetan marriage system very complicated. Heinrich Harrer observed that 'The aristocracy may only marry in their own class and this rule was strictly applied. Relatives may not marry one another except after seven generations, in order to avoid inbreeding. The Dalai Lama alone may permit exceptions to these rules'. More information is available from Dawa Norbu's writings regarding marriage prohibitions in Tibet. In Tibet, people generally married within their own class, caste and religion because it facilitated the individuals getting adjusted easily. The people who belonged to lower caste could marry among themselves. Thus in the past, the Tibetans followed the rule of exogamous marriage.

Regarding age of marriage, there were certain rules. Although in cases of polyandry there was every possibility of age disparity, since all brothers became husbands of the woman to whom their eldest brother was married. Child marriages were very rare in Tibet.

Divorce was not a common feature. But in the event of a divorce, the woman's right was well protected. A divorced wife with her children (mostly sons) was entitled to get one-fourth of the family property. If she had a daughter, she was entitled to get one-sixth of the property. In case one of the children decided to become a monk or nun, the parents had to provide him or her with clothing and provisions. Being monk or nun, they could share their family property and enjoy the proceeds from it. Regarding marriage rituals it did not matter, whether it was polyandrous or a polygamous marriage. The most important was the ritualistic side of the marriage. When it was an arranged marriage, the proposal generally comes from groom's side through a mediator, who was a person, known to both parties. On the basis of a written contract marriage was fixed. The first pre-marital ceremony was the solemnization of marriage which was known as 'Chang' or engagement-ceremony. The family of the groom paid the bride's family sizeable amount of money, which was known as 'Milk Money' (as approximate amount of money spent by the bride's parents for her upbringing). The Groom's parents also had to pay the expenses of the marriage to bride's parents. But this type of contractual marriage was the custom of aristocratic society. To the common people, marriage had no legal or religious contract. Among them it was more simple affair. Among the commoners or aristocracy, astrology and superstition played major role in case of any matrimonial occasion.

## Patterns of Family and Marriage System in Exile

On the basis of the above information available from different literature, a survey was conducted among the selected respondents in India to examine the changing patterns of family structure and consequent changing systems of marriage. As stated earlier, family is the basic social group and is influenced by social and economic condition. In this present study the family of a Tibetan refugee is discussed from the ecological point of view and an attempt has also been made to find out as to what extent the ecological set ups have influenced the family and marriage systems of the Tibetan refugees. So it is imperative to keep in mind the natural environment, because it plays a vital role in determining the structure of the family, besides several socio cultural parameters. In all cases the form and size of social group, the nature of its activities, the trend and limit of its development are strongly influenced by the size and nature of its habitat. The environment indirectly influences the form of family, though its rate of influence varies in accordance with the cultural set up.

Before explaining the changes that have occurred in the family structure and marriage patterns of the Tibetan refugees who arrived in their host country it is important to remember that they came as individuals and not as family or a member of a family. Very few Tibetans could come along with their families. Most of them came alone.

**Table 5: Percentage Distribution of Family Size: Past and Present**

| *Sl.No.* | *Size of the family* | *Past* | | *Present* | |
|---|---|---|---|---|---|
| | | *No. of respondents* | *Percentage* | *No. of respondents* | *Percentage* |
| 1 | 1 to 3 | 18 | 6.54 | 150 | 54.55 |
| 2 | 3 to 5 | 39 | 14.18 | 92 | 33.45 |
| 3 | 5 to 7 | 59 | 21.45 | 25 | 9.1 |
| 4 | 7 to 9 | 7 | 28 | 8 | 2.9 |
| 5 | 10 and above | 82 | 29.82 | nil | nil |
| | | 275 | 100.00 | 275 | 100.00 |

*Source:* Field survey

An overall change is revealed from Table 5 that deals with size and number of family members of the Tibetan refugees in India. It should be mentioned in this context that polyandry is not practiced by the refugees at present. Only a few numbers of families in Sikkim have retained this practice. Also it is very clear that most of the newly emerging nuclear families have been able to come out of their refugee status. As a result, they are gradually adapting to nuclear or conjugal family system.

## The Spread of Modern Education and the Winds of Change

As said earlier according to Tibetan government official statistics, there are about 1,22,078 Tibetans living in different parts of the world. The largest number of them is living in the settlements in South Asia. Out of the total population, 85,000 live in India. So far about 12,153 Tibetans have moved to other parts of the world. USA and Canada has the largest number of Tibetans: the figure has reached up to 7000. Switzerland is the second highest with a Tibetan population of about 2000.

After more than four decades of Chinese occupation of Tibet, the influx of Tibetan refugees continues. An average of 2000 to 2500 Tibetans come India every year. More than 44 percent of them are teenagers and young adults (age 14-25), thirty three percent are adults (age group 26-59), More than 17 percent young children (age group 0-13) and only 5 percent are over the age of sixty.

In order to look after the needs of these refugees, the Tibetan government has opened reception centers in Kathmandu, Delhi and Dharamsala. The young children below the age of 13 years and monks are rehabilitated easily in India by being sent to the schools run by TCV (Tibetan Children Village) and THF and monks and nuns are sent to the monasteries in different refugee settlements. The rehabilitation of adults between the age group 18 and over is a big problem, since many of them are uneducated and unskilled. Tibetan government has set up an adult education centre for these adult/ children where they are taught Basic English, Tibetan language and mathematics as well as arts and crafts. The CTA (Central Tibetan Administration) provides small grants to these adult refugees to start a small business. Many of them are engaged in small antique business and restaurants on the roadside. Initially the Tibetan refugees were engaged in road construction and handicraft. Living a long period in exile they have acquired an occupational adaptability which has been explained in Table 5. The table depicts a comparative analysis of the occupational mode the Tibetans in their homeland as well as in exile. Now they are engaged in business and also a large number of them are employed as professionals. Tibetan refugee community in exile is considered as one of the most successful refugee communities in the world. They have managed to rebuild their lives in a completely alien environment achieving almost total economic self reliance. Tibetan Administration in exile has succeeded in rehabilitating the refugees in a cohesive society creating an environment where Tibetans have been able to preserve their age long rich cultural heritage and identity. Education is playing as an important tool of social mobility. Previously there was no practical education in Tibet and whatever little educational facilities existed were controlled by the religious establishments like monasteries. At present much higher values are being attached to the higher education than the religious education. This change has caused a significant amount of social mobility with a remarkable increase in the number of qualified young Tibetans for professional jobs. In this regard women are no exception. It is interesting to note that the Tibetan women association expressed its views in the Fifth World Conference on Women held in Bejing: 'traditionally the girls in Tibet had fewer educational opportunities' But the girls in exile are equally educated and qualified to that of the boys.

Table 6 explains some interesting features like—after higher secondary level there is an increase in the number of dropouts among the male students. Interviews reveal that this is mainly due to economic reasons. There is a sudden decrease of female students from the graduation level. In this case it is due to social reasons. In most of the cases the girls are getting married during or after graduation. But on the whole at present the younger generation is more interested in modern, western and secular education.

**Table 6: The Status of Education among the Tibetans in exile**

| *Standard of Education* | *No. of Respondent* | *Male* | *Female* |
|---|---|---|---|
| Nil | 15 | 8 | 7 |
| Primary Education | 86 | 56 | 30 |
| High School | 52 | 28 | 24 |
| Higher Secondary | 50 | 29 | 21 |
| University Degree | 59 | 27 | 32 |
| Professional Training/Higher Education | 13 | 10 | 3 |
| Total | 275 | 158 | 117 |

*Source:* Field Survey.

## Social Life and Tibetan Buddhism

Social life in Tibet was totally controlled by the monasteries, because people had to live in accordance with the religious philosophy. It was the duty of the monasteries to make the common people conscious about the religious code, and to regulate their lives according to the religious beliefs. Harrer, observed how religion was present in the life of a commoner. The prayer wheels were constantly rolled, and prayer flags waved on the house tops, tree tops or on the top of the mountains. To the Tibetans, the rain, snow, wind, all sorts' natural phenomena were the various indicators of the presence of God. The divine anger was expressed through hail storm, crop damage, illness or any type of disaster. Potala was the principal centre of religious cum political activities. According to Tibetan belief the highest lamas were the reincarnations of the supreme power, including the Dalai Lamas and the Panchen Lamas, who were at the top of the religious hierarchy. The lower orders in the Lamaistic hierarchy were determined according to the degree of charisma associated with reincarnations. But not all the monks were lamas. The lamas were those whose knowledge of spiritual attainment were fully proved in the various spheres of the monastic life. The Lamas and monks could live under the same roof in the monastery.

In the economic sphere, monasteries were exempted from paying tax. Each and every monastery had its own estate property, they could use all necessary authoritative powers to handle its own affairs, but government could not interfere. Even private trades were allowed inside the monastery. On the basis of income, class hierarchy was maintained inside the monastery, as for example rich monks could own property whereas the poor monks had to serve as servants. Other than income, academic attainments were also taken into consideration for denoting categories of monks, which added another dimension to the hierarchical structure of the monasteries.

On the basis of the above, the lamas were grouped into three categories: a novice, junior monk and full fledged monk. This system of gradation was based on a set of vows that the monks had to take, and were strictly to abide by rules of the sect to which they belonged. To become a 'novice', a lama had to take sixteen vows; 'junior monk' had to take twenty additional vows while a fully fledged monk had to take two hundred and fifty three vows. A senior or full fledged monk could get distinction through intellectual excellence, when a title of 'Geshe' was conferred upon him, which was similar to that of the 'doctorate' degree of the modern Universities.

After attaining highest position in the monastic order lamas could rule over the monastic estate. In other way religion provided power and wealth to the lamas. In the traditional Tibetan society, almost everyone had to take refuge in Buddha, Dharma, Sangha and Lamas, who symbolized the first three, in accordance with the Mahayana belief. When Chinese took over Tibet, Tibetans fled Tibet, mostly to save their religion. They just could not imagine giving up their religious beliefs.

## Socio-religious Life in the Camps

The Chinese atrocities on the Tibetans made them lose contact with their motherland which they left to come to India as destitutes. Particularly the Tibetan Lamas and other religious personnel found their lives in insecure positions. Because it was not possible for them to continue their traditional monasterial way of life in the new ecological set up. Thus, one of the biggest problems for the refugee community and the host administration was how to arrange rehabilitation for a large number of refugee lamas. Realizing fully the value and need of preserving the Tibetan religio-intellectual tradition, some religious institutions were established by the Central Tibetan Administration in which highly intellectual lamas were rehabilitated.

Through Central Tibetan Administration in Dharamsala has been able to succeed in creating traditional religious environment among the refugees, almost all the respondents expressed that they left their country to save their religion. They selected India as their host country because from times immemorial it has been a centre of pilgrimage to them. In India they have got the near homely atmosphere and a secure environment. They have expressed their gratefulness that India has offered them the maximum opportunity to perform their religious rituals and cultural freedom. Among the first generation of refugees thus, religion is the primary concern. They are concerned about the newly emerging socio-economic forces that have already affected the second generation, born and brought up in India, who are in favour of more individualistic and materialistic views.

Since Dalai Lama shifted the headquarters to Dharamsala from Mussoorie in 1960, the place has become a pilgrimage destination to the Tibetans. In India, wherever Tibetan settlements are located the refugees have built the gomphas or monasteries. In these monasteries one can easily observe the traditional rituals being performed by the lamas. The continuous mantras are recited by the refugees. Inside each and every prayer wheel and prayer—cylinder 'Mani-mantsas' are written. It is believed by rotating the wheel once would make one pure for three generations. So these wheels and cylinders are symbol of Tibetan rituals that bring divine merit and satisfaction ritualistic avenue to earn religious merit. The educated Tibetan can earn merit through reading books, but for the uneducated poor man, this is the main path to attain divine merit.

Most of the rituals are related to the birth, death and marriage, which were traditionally practiced in Tibet, are practiced by the refugees in exile. Some modifications have taken place, like butter-oil lamps are replaced by electric bulbs or candles due to economic reasons. 'Kalachakra' is one of the most important 'Tibeto-Buddhist' rituals, and can be delivered by a Dalai Lama, for only a few times during his life time.

Everywhere in India, where the Tibetan settlements are located, one can see prayer flags flying aloft on trees, electric poles or hill tops, from which Tibetan/colonies can be easily recognized. These flags are symbols, which can guarantee long life, material prosperity; moreover they help to drive away evil spirits. These are all traditional Tibetan beliefs. In some of the handicraft centers, the traditional religious paintings are found, which are still being done by the Tibetans. According to their belief, this occupation helps to earn divine merit along with earning money. Even astrology, magic etc. are still practiced by them. Thus the Tibetan refugees in India have been able to maintain or retain the religious essence in their social life despite the drastic changes in ecological set-up. Even in urban areas like New Delhi, (in Majnu-ka-Tilla) it was found, that they have been able to recreate a nucleus of the order of monastic society. They are trying their best to keep alive their cultural heritage. A Tibetan SOS hostel for the Tibetan refugee students has been established in Rohini in New Delhi. The main objectives of this unit are to retain social, cultural and religious heritage among the new generation. For the purpose, students have to attend regular religious lectures and social and cultural functions. They are being regularly made aware of the political development in Tibet by their teachers.

## The Problems of Second Generation Exile

The Tibetan people lived in a unique society in Tibet based on Tibetan Buddhism for more than 1,200 years. Prior to the 1950s, and for more than 350 years, the people of Tibet had lived harmoniously under the spiritual and religious leadership of the successor of Dalai Lama, the incarnation of the Lord Buddha. But, after the Chinese invasion of Tibet in 1950, the Tibetan Buddhist society was reduced to a group of Tibetan followers numbering about 100,000 who escaped across the Himalayas on foot to settle escaped over the Himalayas on foot to settle in refugee camps in India and Nepal.

According to the 1996 World Refugee Survey, about 130,000 Tibetan refugees live in India and Nepal. Everywhere, initially the refugees are subjected to encounter suspicion, commercialism, and the harsh demands for economic survival. In spite of all these they have built several hundred monasteries and nunneries outside Tibet, which help to preserve the Tibetan cultural and religious identity.

The younger generation belong to a modern urban culture. Tibet is considered to be one of the largest serving primitive but stable social orders, which is a balance between agrarian and pastoral social systems. The traditional Tibetan ethos was characterized by a strong synthesis of hierarchy and joint culture by a religion whose chief priest was also the absolute ruler of the country. The overall situation in the traditional Tibetan society was unfavorable ban the emergence of an assertive youth culture. As is stated earlier, there was practically no general education or school in Tibet. Whatever little educational opportunities existed were only limited within the religious institutions, and thus lamas were the only authority. As a result, history says nothing about any conflict between youth power and ruling religious establishments.

Despite these tough conditions, many of the first and second generation of Tibetan refugees including the Dalai Lama himself, believe Tibet as mother earth and homeland. Inspired by the Buddhist teaching, they continue to use nonviolent means of agitation in their struggle for recovering their homeland. However, many members of the third generation of exiles, born and raised in India, Nepal or in elsewhere , hardly share the older generations' concern of maintaining the Tibetan identity. The youth's mood has undergone a dramatic change in the emigrant Tibetan community, in India; because in the refugee life the youth have been exposed to an entirely different environment. They can hardly see a specific vision for their future as Tibetan in exile. Many tend to lose patience with the nonviolent struggle; thus they simply express their nationalistic and patriotic feelings, consisting primarily of strong hatred for the Chinese Communist government. They have hardly nourished their emotional and religious attachment to their lost homeland and its traditional culture of Tibetan Buddhism like first and second generations. At the same time, consumer-culture attracts them. These grandchildren of exiles tend to assimilate, losing their unique religio-cultural identity as Tibetans in daily life. Thus Tibetan Buddhism seems to increasingly give way to westernized consumer culture in their new host countries.

Thus the new generation has thus suddenly been caught in a vortex of change. Statistics show that approximately fifty percent of the Tibetans in exile are in 25-35 age group. This means that the composition of the Tibetan population in exile is changing from an older generation of hard working but unskilled people to a multilingual generation born and brought up in an entirely different environment. The younger generation can only inherit the culture and language. The youth who has grown up in India are mentally and spiritually different from those in the past. It is not expected from a young Tibetan would accept all rigid conventions of the older generation. Thus a new type of adolescent mentality is observed among the younger generation. As such the older generations are feeling some sort of concern at the rapid and rather traumatic changes among the educated young Tibetan refugees. Sometimes they are afraid of the cherished aims that the group has set for itself are at stake. To the older Tibetans, they had to leave their homeland, only to save their culture and religion, now it poses to them another problem as how they would be able to preserve their culture and religion against this new challenge.

Thus, in conclusion it can be said from the study that most of the Tibetan refugees fled from their land to save their religion and culture. But there is a clear tendency towards differentiation between sacred and the secular spheres of social life, which was absent in the traditional culture in Tibet. A significant change in traditional class structure is also found. In the traditional Tibetan society, social, political and religious hierarchies merged into one another. The absence of this traditional social hierarchy in India had led to the emergence of ideological trends, which are entirely new in the Tibetan refugee society.

## REFERENCES

1. Richard Bell, Charles, *Tibet Past and Present*, Oxford, 1924.
2. Macdonald, David, *The Land of the Lama,* London, 1929.
3. Richardson, Hugh, *Tibet and Its History*, London, 1962.
4. *Amer. Acad. Polit. Soc. Sc.* Nov. 1961, p. 338.

5. Aziz, Barbara Nimri, *Tibetan Frontier Families: Reflections From Three Generations from D'ing-ri*, New Delhi, Vikas Publishing House Pvt Ltd, 1978.
6. Avedon, J., *In Exile from the Land of Snows*: *The Definitive Account of the Dalai Lama and Tibet Since the Chinese Conquest,* Alfred A Knopf, Inc, 1984.
7. Bell, Charles, *The People of Tibet*, Oxford, 1928.
8. Banerjee, B.N., *India's Aid to its Neighbouring Countries*, New Delhi, 1982.
9. Ray Burma, Bina, *Religion and Politics in Tibet*, New Delhi, 1979.
10. Chand, Attar, *Tibet Past & Present* (1660-1981), New Delhi, 1982.
11. Das, Sarat Chandra. *Contributions on the Religion & History of Tibet* New Delhi, 1970.
12. Dargyay, Eva. K., *Tibetan Village Community: Structure and Change,* New Delhi, Vikas Publishing House Pvt Ltd, 1982.
13. Dalai Lama, *Freedom in Exile: The Autobiography of the Dalai Lama of Tibet*. London: Hodder & Stoughton, 1990.
14. Norbu, Dawa, *Tibet-The Road Ahead*, London: Rider, 1987.
15. Norbu, Dawa, 'The state of Tibetan education', *Tibetan Review*, 11 (4), 1976, pp. 3-4.
16. Dawa, T. S., 'Bad teachers make good ones ineffective', *Tibetan Review*, 21 (6) 21, 1986
17. De Voe, 'Keeping Refugee Status: A Tibetan perspective', in Scott, M.M. and Elizabeth Colson (eds.), *People in upheaval*, New York: Center for Migration Studies, 1987.
18. Dodd, T., 'Refugee Education: The Case for International Action', in *Report of an International Workshop on Refugee Education* (Dartington, Devin, England, March 29 to April 1, 1985) ED283393.
19. E.J.B. Rose, *Color and Citizenship: a Report on British Race Relations*, London: Oxford University Press, 1969.
20. Gupta, Manu Rani, *Social Mobility and change among Tibetan Refugees*, New Delhi: Raj Publications, 2005.
21. Hope, Simpson, *The Refugee Problem*, Oxford University Press, 1939.
22. Harrer, Heinrich, *Seven Years in Tibet,* London, 1953.
23. Jones, C. and Rutter, J. *Refugee Education*, England: Trentham Books Limited, 1998.
24. Kalsang, Tenzin, 'Problems of Tibetan Education', *Tibetan Review,* 21 (8), 1986, pp. 11-12.
25. Labeisse, 'The Paradox of Tibetan education in exile', *Tibetan Review,* 30 (8), 1995, pp. 18-20.

26. Lhasang Tsering (1986), 'Education of Tibetans in India: Some suggested changes', *Tibetan Review*, 21 (2).
27. Norbu, Dawa, *Red Star Over Tibet*, London, 1974.
28. Matza, David, 'Subterranean Traditions of the Youth', *Annals of the American Academy of Political Science,* Vol. 338, November 1961.
29. Muni S.D. and Baral Raj Lok, 'Refugees and Regional Security in South Asia', RCSS and Konark Publications, New Delhi, 1996.
30. Norbu, Dawa, 'Tibetan Refugees from Tibet: A Structural Causes of Successful Settlement', in S.K. Roy (ed), Refugees and Human Rights, Rawat Publications, New Delhi, 2001.
31. Patterson, George N., *Tibet in Revolution*, London, 1960.
32. Ray Burman, Bina, *Religion and Politics in Tibet*, New Delhi: Vikas, 1979.
33. Richardson, *Tibetans in Exile—Tibet and its History*, Oxford University Press, London, 1962.
34. Sinha N.C., *An Introduction to the History and Religion of Tibet*, Calcutta, 1975.
35. Saklani, Girija, *The Uprooted Tibetans in India*, New Delhi, 1984.
36. Stein, R.A., *Tibetan Civilization*. London, 1972.
37. Samaddar, Ranabir, *Refugees and the State: Practices of Asylum and Care in India, 1946-2000*, Sage Publication India Private Limited, New Delhi, 2003.
38. Thomas Lowell, *The Silent War in Tibet*, New York, 1959.
39. *Tibetan Review*, Vol. XXI, No. 6, June 1986.
40. *Tibetan Review*, Vol. XXVIII, No. 1, January 1993.
41. *Tibetan Review*, Vol. XXI, No. 8, August 1986.
42. *Tibetan Review*, Vol. XXV, No. 2, February 1990.
43. *Tibetan Review*, Vol. I, No. 9, September 1960.
44. *Tibetan Review*, Vol. XXVIII, No. 6, June 1993.
45. *Tibetan Review*, Vol. XXIV, No. 12, Dec. 1986.
46. *Tibetan Review*, Vol. XXIV, No. 9, 1989.
47. Waddell. L.A., *The Buddhism of Tibet or Lamaism*. London 1959.

# 5

# RAHULA SANKRITYAYANA AND BUDDHISM: A COMPLEX ENGAGEMENT

*Maya Joshi*

## Introduction

Mahapandita Rahula Sankrityayana offers a fascinating and thought-provoking perspective into the question of the relevance of Buddhist ideas in the contemporary world. His multi-faceted life embraced many roles: traveler, translator, historian, activist and prolific writer in many genres and languages. His life was at one level singular, even eccentric. Yet he connected in vital ways with the dominant issues of the times and places he inhabited, wrestling with the problems he and his contemporaries sought to define and seek solutions to.

Within this frame of a life of ceaseless activity, both physical and intellectual, his engagement with Buddhism was of special interest and value, as even a casual acquaintance with his life and works confirms. Even his chosen name, the last and most lasting of several that he adopted to mark his journey through life, owes its origins to his conversion to Buddhism as a young man. His more substantial and lasting contribution to Buddhist Studies followed. Besides his work as a teacher of Buddhist philosophy—in ochre robes and in lay garb, inside the academy and outside it—he is perhaps best known for voyaging into Tibet in search of rare Buddhist manuscripts and artifacts, and for editing and restoring substantial parts of the rich Buddhist heritage preserved there. Though often working quite independently, he was in line with a world-wide trend amongst Indologists and Buddhist scholars to recreate the lost Buddhist heritage protected and enriched in Tibet in the centuries subsequent to the sack of great ancient universities of Nalanda and Vikramshila.

However, Rahula-ji, as he is often called, brought to his engagement with Buddhism more than his considerable linguistic and scholarly abilities. He embraced Buddhism as he did the other ideologies that he encountered: with the full force of an intellect and life responsive to the social and political currents of the time. In this paper, I propose to use his multi-volume autobiography, *Meri Jeevan Yatra*, in conjunction with his essays and biographical writings, to arrive at an understanding of the dynamics of Rahul Sankrityayana's engagement with Buddhism. It is a journey that juxtaposes philosophical ideas with urgent political tensions and forces a review of Buddhism's relevance within a world of contesting historical pulls and pressures.

## The Life

A brief sketch of the major events of Rahula-ji's life shows the broad patterns of his philosophical growth. Born Kedarnath Pandey in 1893 to an orthodox Brahmin family in Azamgarh village in the state of Uttar Pradesh, it was only in 1930 that he acquired the full name and title that he died with and is still largely known by: Mahapandita

Rahula Sankrityayana. In the intervening period, he studied and experimented with many philosophies and paths in an ever-widening search for a truth that answered his many-hued engagement with the world and its crises. He had a spell as a Hindu sadhu by the name of Baba Ram Udaar Das in 1912-13, during which he had been offered the *mahant*-hood of Vaishnava Parsa *Math* in Bihar. He soon fled this *math* as he found the feudal lifestyle and his inability to continue his Sanskrit studies while there repellent and started traveling through India on foot. He went to the South of India, studying Sanskrit at the Vaishnava Math at Tirumishi, and yet again declined a chance to be heir to the *math*. He left Tirumishi and took his next step away from Hindu orthodoxy, which took place after a rather unpleasant taste of that orthodoxy. In 1914 he was beaten up by orthodox Shaivite *sadhus* for opposing animal sacrifice at a temple in Ayodhya. He then joined the Hindu reformist movement called the Arya Samaj in 1914, continuing his study of Sanskrit and Logic, while also getting inspired by the nationalist/anti-imperialist streak of the Arya Samaj. As an Arya Samaji proselytiser, he wrote articles under the name Kedarnath Vidyarthi, and also came in contact with Buddhist ideas. It was during his visit to Nepal in 1923, followed by the one to Sri Lanka in 1927, that he systematically studied Buddhism, acquiring the title of Tripitikacharya at the Vidyalankara Perivena, the leading monastic college in Sri Lanka. Teaching Sanskrit and learning Pali at Vidyalankara, he faced yet another philosophical crisis and finding, after due deliberation, that belief in a soul, or *atman,* was insupportable as an idea, formally declared his abandonment of the 'Hindu' tradition and became a Buddhist. Having Urdu, Hindi, Sanskrit, Arabic and Persian and of course his native Bhojpuri already at his command, he had by now acquired a knowledge of Pali, Singhalese and Tibetan. Convinced of the need to study Buddhism in a wider frame, and inspired by the lost glory of the Nalanda tradition, he traveled to Tibet four times, in disguise, and at considerable personal risk from the double hazard of ruthless local bandits and the British Police, and brought back with him over 1600 Buddhist manuscripts and texts on mule, translating some of them along the way.

While his titles (Mahapandita and Tripitakacharya) indicate his mastery of Sanskrit and Pali texts, the name 'Rahul' was chosen for its Buddhist antecedents (being the name of Prince Siddhartha Gautama's son) and 'Sankrityayana' was crafted in recognition of the gotra that his family belonged to. This curiously composite name of his own invention (Buddhist and residually Brahmanical in its inclusion of the caste category) served him through his visits to Europe as a Buddhist missionary in 1932, during which period he declined, on political grounds, an invitation to travel to America in the same role. The name stayed with him in his later overtly Socialist phase which started in the late 30s, augmented by his visit to the USSR, where he learnt Mongolian and Russian, and taught Buddhist philosophy at Leningrad University at the invitation of the renowned scholar of Buddhist Logic, Tscherbatsky. In 1937, 1944 and 1962, he revisited the USSR, the last time tragically for treatment for amnesia. In between he returned to and traveled extensively in India, participating actively in the nationalist movement, especially in activities of the Kisan Sabha and the Indian National Congress. His nationalist political involvement earned him several jail terms, which he effectively utilized to further his education and produce much of his voluminous oeuvre. In 1939, disillusioned with the Congress in Bihar, he became a member of the Communist Party of India and stayed a member for nine years before having his membership cancelled in 1948 for his controversial defense of the Hindi language as "Rashtrabhasha", which was perceived to be partisan and majoritarian by fellow comrades. Subsequently, he rejoined the Communist Party in 1955, and spent the last phase of his life in Darjeeling, where he passed away in 1963, the last few years of his life spent in spells of writing and teaching on Marxist and Buddhist themes while simultaneously battling a debilitating amnesia.

This quick sketch captures very little indeed of Rahula Sankrityayana's place and significance which can be gauged somewhat better by the variety and volume of the written and translated work he left behind in Hindi, Bhojpuri and Tibetan. These range from nine novels, four collections of short stories, an autobiography published originally in five volumes, fifteen biographies of religious and political leaders, ranging from "Stalin" to "Mahamanav Buddha", twelve travelogues of travels across Asia and Europe, with many through remote Himalayan states, seven collections of essays, ten translated books, and several little booklets on science, sociology, politics, philosophy, religion, and folklore in Hindi alone. Apart from this there are three primers on the Tibetan language, two Bhojpuri plays, and last, but certainly not the least, fifteen volumes of classical Buddhist texts that he researched, edited, and translated.

## The Buddhist Rahul: Issues and Continuities with Marxism

As told in *Meri Jeevan Yatra*, a multi-volume account of his various travels, literal and metaphorical, an important point in this narrative of growth is the encounter with, conversion to, and movement away from Buddhism. It is also a narrative that is interlaced with the political and social reality of an emergent nation, attempting to forge its identity as it fights colonial exploitation. It is important to remember that Rahula-ji's engagement with philosophy as such is increasingly coloured by a growing involvement with the anti-colonial nationalist struggle, and more specifically, with a certain group which seeks to represent the rights of India' poorest, amongst them the peasants of Bihar, his chosen *karmabhoomi*. The addition of this class-angle to his analysis of the ills of Indian society has a dual effect: it both draws him towards Buddhism and also finally takes him away from it.

What appears as the final conclusion was this scholar-traveller found it necessary to travel 'beyond' Buddhism to arrive at Marxism—a philosophy and a practice that many today would see as being the very polar opposite of Buddhism. At the same time, his continued scholarly interest in Buddhist studies till the very end of his life, a vocation that required a considerable exercise of physical and mental labour, often involving considerable personal risk, both physical and financial, seems to refute this argument. At the end of his life as a complex person—politically Marxist, but committed scholastically and academically to the cause of Buddhist Studies to the very end of his days in 1963, and confessing to a deep *shraddha* for the figure of the Buddha despite his Marxist doctrinaire distancing from it as early as the 30s.

The philosophical links between Buddhism and Marxism did not escape this relentless traveler in the realms of thought. Indeed, it is precisely in the closeness of Buddhism to Marxism that Rahula Sankrityayana finds meaning in it. This necessarily involves an emphasis which underplays the ritual aspect of Buddhism in favour of the rational 'philosophy', that teases out the Dharma's collectivist possibilities over the focus on individual salvation, and finds value in those aspects of it that are outward-looking and socially engaged rather than inward-looking, meditative or promotive of detachment from the world. And, in so far as Buddhism has deviated historically from these 'desirables'—of being theoretically conducive to social change, collective good and rational thinking—he feels free to criticize it as an inadequate answer to contemporary problems.

Rahul's first encounter with Buddhism, in his own telling, was steeped in ignorance wrought of generations of collective historical amnesia. The educated Indian class's new-found appreciation of Buddhism, visible since the early 20$^{th}$ century, he points out somewhat sardonically, is actually a reunion with its lost soul which owes much to the academic interest of Western scholars, especially the Russians, followed by the French and the Germans. (*Bhadant Bodhananda Mahastavir*, pp. 402-3) It was only in 1910, when he reached Bareilly after completing his first courageous trip to Badrinath, that he received a somewhat clearer exposition of Buddhism in the form of a pamphlet in Sanskrit by a Sadhu Khunnilal Shastri. Much later, in his Arya Samaji phase, he heard more about the liberal views of the Buddhists, which ironically had the effect of rousing this hitherto zealous Arya Samaji's curiosity in that rival faith. Subsequently, meeting the Buddhist monk Bodhananda Mahasthavir, he started an intellectual engagement with Buddhism which took him first to Sri Lanka, and then to Tibet, bringing him in close contact with the Bhikshus Jagdish Kashyap and Ananda Kausalyayana, with whom he made common cause for the restoration of Buddhism's lost glory in the land of its birth.

Buddhism also reinforced his favored philosophy of "ghumakkari", a life devoted to ceaseless wandering as a mode of learning and teaching. His fascinating little book *Ghumakkar Shastra* considers the various religious traditions that have fostered this path; Christianity, Brahmanism, and Islam, all three acquire a greater degree of tolerance when a *ghumakkar* truly devoted to the path takes to these religions. But Buddhism is the gem amongst them all, due to its radical freedom from the caste ridden purity/pollution taboos that prevent a free mixing of human beings and render the traveller's enterprise difficult and sometimes impossible. It is only in the Buddhist tradition that a Mongol and an Indian face, or an Asian or a European complexion, created no possibilities of discrimination, he asserts, on the basis of historical evidence, he argues. Quite contrary to the insulating effect of the Brahaminical taboos on travel across the oceans, Buddhism encourages the spread of its rational and universal message via travel through the most difficult terrains, its missionaries heroically transcending all obstacles, be they the mighty Himalayas or the Gobi desert. (*Bhadant Bodhanand Mahasthavir*, p. 403)

The philosophical basis for this high regard for the Buddha lay in his appreciation of the sophistication of Buddhist philosophy, in its foundational concepts such as *pratitya samutpada* (dependent origination), *kshanikavada* (momentariness), and *anatmavada* (theory of no-self). In *Ateet se Vartaman* (1956) a very Marxist Rahul explicates Buddhist concepts, silencing critics that Buddhism is not a full-fledged philosophy. True to his commitment to the common man, he explains complex philosophical ideas such as the theory of Momentarines and the Middle Path in lay man's terms and demonstrates Buddhism's relevance to the real world. In the process, he also shows how close it is to Marxist Dialectical Materialism.

In his essay on "Buddhist Dialectics" (*Buddhism: The Marxist Approach*, 1970), he explains the continuities between Buddhism and Marxism: it is easier for someone with a Buddhist background to understand Marxist philosophy, he says, linking the dialectical method in Buddhism, its rejection of a creator god, and its human-centred approach with some Marxist ideas. He cites Buddhism's 'irrationalities' as a point of departure between the two.

In *Darshan Digdarshan*, he uses Marxist terminology to critique Buddhism's historically status quoist character, whereby despite its philosophical commitment to a radically dynamic order, its openness to marginalized groups and castes, it compromised with the interests of the ruling classes and under pressure from King Bimbisara, The Buddha made rules for the *sangha* that excluded runaway soldiers and slaves, thus protecting the interest of those who employed them. There are moments in Rahul where he, like D.P. Chattopadhyay and D.D. Kosambi, accepts Buddhism's role in challenging orthodoxy and bringing about social change; indeed it becomes a form of primitive communism, but he concludes that "the time" was not right for the Buddha's radical philosophical ideas to be historically realized.

Significantly, Rahula's writings on Buddhism do not emphasise what might call psychological inner work through meditative practice. Himself a *karmayogi*, rather than a *dhyanayogi*, he focuses, on the public implications of Buddhist ideas. He focuses on the least arcane, the most universally and easily understood, of the Buddha's teachings. The Buddha is for him a realist-humanist:

> He wants the good of all beings—'*sabbe satta bhavantu sukhi tatta'*. But he was not a passive dreamer. He was a realist. Thus when he instructed his disciples to set out to work, inspiring them to propagate the dharma, he did not say to them they should direct their efforts to the good of all beings; rather he said that they should travel far and wide for the good of the many ("*bahujan hitaya, bahujan sukhaya*"). He knew, that the good of the many is sometimes contrary to the interests of some. Society is divided along opposing interests. In his view, the way primitive man consumed worldly goods was the ideal mode of consumption. ("Buddha aur Gandhi", in *Rahula Vangmaya, 2.2: Jeevani aur Sansmaran*, p. 426, my translation)

As the above excerpt clarifies, for Sankrityayana, Buddhism's significance lies in its proximity to ideals of an egalitarian social order that did not shy away from the practical problems of making such an order a concrete reality. Poised at the point of history that he was, and having first taken *sanayas* in the Hindu tradition and then having been and Arya Samaji nationalist, Buddhism was for him the next point of arrival, combining as it did the possibility of social work and a growing disinclination for belief in a Creator. His distinction between 'the good of all' and 'the good of the many' serves to highlight the centrality of class conflict. This growing conviction was fed no doubt by his involvement in the (Peasant's Struggle) of feudal Bihar, a sub-struggle within the larger national freedom struggle, a move that turned him away from Gandhiji's mainstream Congress movement, which he found riddled with elitism, especially in Bihar, where one of the worst oppressors of poor peasants was an elected Congress candidate: a feudal landlord. The 1917 revolution in Russia had had a profound impact on him, and it was therefore perhaps inevitable that he should become later a card-carrying Communist, underscoring the belief that struggle is often the only means of achieving a just social order.

## By Way of a Conclusion

Sankrityayana's life, in its creative and passionate engagement with the complex reality of the dynamic world as he encountered it, especially with ideas that sought to explain and change that world, becomes a multi-coloured prism to examine questions of Buddhism's place and relevance. His own relevance today, is a linked enquiry that places the question of Buddhism's relevance in a context that is alive with the real tensions—ideological and historical—that beset the world he lived in, a formative part of India's life in the early decades of the last century. Buddhism, like Marxism later, each with its own kind of concomitant internationalism and universalism, saturated Rahula-ji's life and thought and formed the crux of his vocational concerns after he left the Arya Samaj and formally took initiation in Buddhism. The questions he asked still demand a close and hard look: how far has humanity progressed in finding solutions to the problems that engaged Rahula-ji, and how may Buddhism, in its many manifestations today, address these concretely.

### REFERENCES

Kashyap, Bhikshu Jagadish, "*Rahulaji: Mere Gurubhai*", in *Rahula Smriti*, Ramsharan Sharma 'Munshi' and Pushpamala Jain (eds.), New Delhi: People's Publishing House, 1988.

Singh, Namvar, "*Kedar se Rahul*," in *Rahula Vangamaya - 1.1: Jeevan Yatra*, 1944.

Sankrityayana, Rahula, "*Bhadant Bodhananda Mahasthavir*," in *Rahul Vangmaya - 2.2: Jeevani Sansmaran*, Delhi: Radhakrishna Prakashan, pp. 402-406.

______ *Buddha Charya* (1931, Kashi Vidyapeeth), Lucknow: Bharatiya Bauddha Samiti, 1995 (third edition).

______ "Buddhist Dialectics", in *Buddhism: The Marxist Approach* (1970), New Delhi: People's Publishing House, 1990.

______ *Ghumakkar Shastra* (1948), Allahabad: Kitab Mahal, 1957.

______ *Meri Jeevan Yatra, Vols. I* (1944), *II* (1950), *III &IV* (1967), Delhi: Radhakrishna Prakashan, reprint, 2005.

# 6

# Concept of Revenue Generation in Buddhist Literature

*Madhumita Chattopadhyay*

A state cannot perform its activities properly without money. Kauṭilya very aptly has said that finance is the basis for starting all the activities of a state—"*kośapūrvāḥ sarvāraṁbhāḥ*". This holds true not only for the Hindu states but also for the Buddhist ones. In the Aśokāvadānaṃ it is stated that the power of a king lies in state treasury: *koṣabalinaścarājānaḥ*.[1] In the *Aggañña Sutta* of the *Dīgha Nikāya*, where the origin of kingship has been discussed in details, we get an idea of revenue system in germicidal form. There it is stated that when the people decided to select a person among themselves, who will look after their fields so that the crops are not stolen by anybody, and whom they regarded as *mahājanasammata* or as *rājā*, they planned to offer him one-sixth of the crops generated. This means that they were ready to submit one-sixth portion of their harvest to the king as revenues in lieu of the service they received from the king, namely protection and maintenance of their individual lands. This story not only gives us an idea of the origin of state administration, but at the same time, provides an account for tax submission, even though there is no mention of any clear-cut principle for tax system. Not only in *Dīgha Nikāya*, but also in other sources of Buddhist literature, it is possible to get the idea that the Buddhists also recognised the importance of revenue earning for the maintenance of a state.

Regarding the principle of taxation, there are lots of discussions in the *Arthaśāstra* and in the *Mahābhārata*. In the *Mahābhārata* in one of the discourses Bhîma has advised that an intelligent king should settle the taxes on the analogy of a calf. Just as a calf, when given proper nourishment, grows strong and becomes able to endure fatigue, and when not fed properly, cannot grow enough to serve any purpose, a kingdom overburdened with taxation will not be able to serve any great purpose. So, the king is advised to earn the taxes in the manner of a bee. Just as bees suck honey from every flower little by little, similarly the king should take little by little from his subjects, leaving something for their own sustenance. Analogy of bees collecting honey is offered in the Buddhist texts also for suggesting the king's method of collecting taxes. In the text *Divyāvadāna*, though it belongs to a later period, the king is advised by his good ministers thus: "Kingdoms, O Lord! are like flowers and plants and fruit-trees; just as flourishing plants and fruit trees being nourished properly yield flowers and fruits at the proper season, so the kingdoms being protected yield taxes and revenues."[2] So, from all these it can be said that in the Buddhist period the maxims connected with revenue earnings were as follows:

(a) taxes should not be a burden to the tax-bearers; there should be ample amount for their own subsistence.
(b) taxes, if necessary, are to be increased gradually in almost imperceptible degrees and not all in a lump.
(c) this increase is to be made at time and place when it is most suitable for the tax-payers.[3]

In a nutshell, the revenue earning should always be subject-friendly and not the ruler-friendly.

Revenue from the land was the chief source of income of the State. Land-tax was considered to be the share of the kingdom from the products of the land (*raññobhāga*) and was technically known as '*bali*'. In the *Pāli* Buddhist Literature the terms '*bali*' and '*bhāga*' were used to mean revenue earned from lands. The term '*bali*' is also found in the orthodox literature like the *Arthaśāstra* of Kautilya or the *Mahābhārata*, but the sense in which the term is used there is different from the sense in which it is used in the Buddhist literature. In the orthodox literature the term seems to mean a different kind of tax, perhaps a religious one. It often stands for any offering a propitiatory oblation, like an offering of portions of food, such as grain, rice etc. to certain goods, semi-divine beings, spirits, man, animals, birds and other creatures including even lifeless objects.[4] But in the Buddhist literature it stands for the king's share from the land. But, how much share the king should get from the land has not been specified in clear terms. The general rate was one-sixth. However, in normal times, it often varied as one-twelfth, one-tenth, one-eighth, one-sixth but in emergency situation it often came to one-fourth, and even one-third. This variation in rate was made in proportion to the cost of cultivation, amount of product, condition of market and the nature of soil. Normally, this was the situation when the king was just and equitable. But when the king was not so the rate depended mostly on his whims. Generally, though not always, this '*bali*' was paid in kind.

In the Buddhist society, the land as a whole was considered to be divided in separate farm-holdings, to be possessed by individual farmers or villagers. From the product of each farm-holding, the king was to be given his share (*bhāga*). How much share the king was entitled to obtain was determined by some pre-existing rule prevalent in that society. From the inscription of Asoka, it is also evident that land revenue was one of the main sources of the state's earning. In the Lumbini Pillar Inscription, there is mention of the *bhāga* or the share of the land-produce payable to the government and *bali* a religious cess as the source of income of the state. In one of the *Jātaka* stories, namely *Kāmajātaka*, procedure for assessment of *bhāga* has been stated. There it is said that a prince renounced his claim to the throne for his younger brother, came to a village and stayed as a guest in a merchant's family. The royal officers (*Rājakammikkā*) came to the village to measure the fields including those belonging to the merchant. The merchant requested the prince to write to the king for remission of *bali* and the prince accordingly did so. Seeing this, other villagers also approached the prince to ask for the reduction of the amount of *bali* on their part too, and as the prince made the request it was granted. This story shows that at the time of fixing *bali*, the process was thus: first the land was measured by a royal official and then on the basis of that measurement a certain amount of *bali* was assessed. This further implies the existence of an already existing standard rate set by the government for a known unit area, which was applied at the time of assessment of the land possessed by an individual. A description of how a land was measured is provided in the *Kurudhamma Jātaka*. There it is said that a royal officer called *rajjugāhaka amacco* (an officer who holds the rope/cord to measure a land) ties a cord to a stick and gives one end to the owner of the field and takes the other end himself. Seeing a crab hole at the spot where he wants to fix the stick he was worried. Fixing it in the hole might kill the crab which violates the principle of non-violence. To avoid it, if he puts the stick in front of the hole, he would cause loss to the king's revenue, while if he were to put it behind the hole, he would cause loss to the cultivator. This story indicates that the official measurement of a land was connected with the assessment of revenue earned from the land. It also implies the existence of standard rates of such land-revenue for measured unit-areas.

In the same story we also get the idea of standard rates of land-revenue for known units. It is said there that a rich man (*seṭṭhhi*) went to his paddy field one day and saw a head of rice bursting the husk. He went about to tie it up with a wisp of rice. He unwittingly took a handful of rice while tying the head to a post with some wisps. This incident made him very remorseful for he thought that he had not yet given the king his due but had taken a handful of rice from that field, which was against the rules of *Kuru* righteousness. This idea of his violating the *Kurudhamma* indicates that there was a method of appraising the standard crops grown from a land.

There is also mention of another official, namely the Master of the Granaries, who was known as *droṇamāpaka*, as he used to measure grain with *droṇa*. His task was to measure the royal share of corn (*rājabhāga*) while sitting at the door of the royal granary. One day one such *droṇamāpaka* was sitting at the door of the granary and measuring the grains. He took a handful of grain from the heap which had not yet been measured and put it down as marker. However, at that moment it started raining and the official counted the markers and dropped them on the heap that had already been measured. When he rushed inside he could not remember whether he had thrown the markers on the measured heap or the unmeasured one. He was disturbed because if the markers were thrown on the heap that had already been measured, the king's property would increase at the cost of the individual owner's share. This story evidently points to the method how the crops used to be divided at the king's granary on the basis of individual's share of crops harvested.[5] This story of the *droṇamāpaka*, who was also known as *Mahāmātta* indicates the fact that at the time of the *Jātakas*, the *droṇamāpaka* was the chief collector of land-revenues and he was subordinate to the *sannidhātā*, the finance minister who used to look after the treasury and the store houses.

From these stories we also get an account of the method of collection of land revenue during the Buddhist period. Lands were surveyed and divided into separate plots known as *pratyayas*. In this connection it may be noted that the earliest reference to land-survey is found in the *Jātakas*.[6] These plots or *pratyayas* were measured by *rajjugāhaka-amācca* who used to assess the land and settle the king's share. The crops cultivated in the plots could not be gathered before the king's portion was assessed. And finally, the king's portion were collected under the supervision of the *droṇamāpaka mahāmāttas* and put in the royal granary. This shows that land-revenue at that time was submitted in the form of crops produced in the land.

These two officers, namely the *rajjugāhaka-amācca* and the *droṇamāpaka mahāmāttas* held responsible positions in respect of land-revenue collection. *Rajjugāhaka* was the chief provincial revenue officers connected mainly with survey, land settlement and irrigation and the *droṇamāpakas* were subordinate to such revenue officers. They also held important and influential positions, connected directly with revenue collectors.[7]

It may be noted in this context that all the revenue earned from a land was not enjoyed by the king only, some portions were enjoyed by a particular individual, namely the headman of the village, who was known as *gāmabhojaka* and the village was known as *bhogagāma*. The *gāmabhojaka* used to enjoy the revenue received from the village and that is why the king's officers did not visit those villages for collecting revenues from them. This suggests that these *bhogagāmas* were grants, endowments or assignments given as reward of merit or as an act of favour from the king. The revenue earned for such land was thus enjoyed by the particular individual, the *gāmabhojaka,* and may be he had to pay a certain portion of their income to the government.[8]

In spite of there being definite laws for collecting land revenues, the situation was not so simple and the collectors used to torment people to a great extent in the name of collecting taxes. These tax-collectors were called '*balisādhakas*', '*balipatiggāhakas*', '*niggāhakas*', '*tuṇdiyas*' and '*ākāsiyas*'. In Buddhist literature, these people were never praised and, on the contrary, it is found that people used the bitterest words against them. This was because of the fact that these officials tried to collect taxes more than what was usual from the poor earnings of the cultivators. In *Gaṇḍatindu Jātaka* there is a narrative of the conditions of the ordinary people under the pressure of the king's officers. King *Pañcāla* of the kingdom of *Kampilla* ruled his kingdom unrighteously. The king being unrighteous all his ministers became the same. The king's officers used to pressurise people with unnecessary taxes and the subjects were oppressed by taxation. Out of fear of the king's officials, they did not dare to stay in their own houses during the day time. With their wives and family they wandered in the forests like wild beasts. During the night time, they used to come back home for fear of burglary, and at daybreak they would disappear once again in the forest. In a *gāthā* of the same *Jātaka* the feelings of the people are recorded:

> "By night to thieves a prey are we, to publicans by day,
> Lewd folks abound within the realm, when evil kings bear sway.
> Distrest by such a fear as this, men to the forest flee,
> And round their dwellings scatter thorns, for their security."[9]

Such a story points to the oppressive measures that used to be employed for collecting revenues or taxes from the poor people. The condition of the poor people under such oppression has been described in the *Jātakas* as being crushed like sugarcane in a mill[10] so that they could not lift their heads.[11] In contrast to this, there were occasions when the village people were exempted from taxes or the amount of tax to be paid was reduced. Such incidences happened when the king was pleased. From the rock edicts of King *Aśoka* it is known that in the case of *Lumbini*, *Aśoka* reduced the land-revenue to one-eighth portion of the crops generated, and totally exempted the village from the payment of the religious cess. This foregoing of all taxes and duties were gesture of royal favour to his subjects.[12]

Though not explicitly stated, there are hints in the Buddhist literature which suggest the existence of property taxes. In the Buddhist society an important class was constituted by the *gahapatis*, who were considered to be one of the seven treasures of a righteous ruler. These *gahapatis* were prized and valued possession of an emperor, representing the economy without which the whole sovereignty would fall like castles of cards. Such *gahapatis* had in their possessions large assets consisting of land, orchards, corn, cattle, slaves, gold and silver. Because of possessing such assets they had to pay taxes to the king. In the *Digha Nikāya* the *gahapati* is described as someone who 'pays taxes and thus increases the wealth of the king—*gahapatiko, kārakārakarâisvaḍḍhako*'.[13] From this it can be inferred that property tax was prevalent in the Buddhist society and an important portion of the state's revenue was generated from such taxes.

Trade and commerce were also sources of income. In the *Mahābodhi Jātaka*, while pointing to the distinction between righteous and unrighteous ruling by a king, it has been stated that when a warrior king follows an unrighteous path, the disaster would be throughout the country and, as a consequence, there would be a loss in trade as well:

> So should he spoil his citizens so apt by trade to gain,
> A Failing sources of revenue will his exchequer drain[14]

These lines indicate that trade was also an important source of revenue of the state, but it failed to yield its usual result when the whole kingdom was under the sway of an unrighteous king. The king could also gain money from trade by fixing taxes on the merchants who came from other places for trading. Traders had to pay first octroi duties for all the objects which were imported in the town and villages at different rates. The state justified these duties on the ground that the money earned was to be utilised for the maintenance of roads through which the merchandise was carried. However, there was no fixed rate at which such duty was to be collected. Fixing the taxes depended on the will of the king. If the king was just, he would levy the taxes on mercantile objects in a reasonable way enabling the trade market to prosper, but it was not so if the king was unjust. In the *Saṃvara Jātaka*, there is the story of prince Samvara who was instructed by the *Bodhisatva* to follow the righteous way of a king. Being guided by such instruction, he fixed just and equitable taxes on the merchants and, as a result, he won the merchant folks and traders to his side. In the text *Divyāvadāna*, the time of which is assumed to be the third century B.C., there are three stories which speak of the existence of tolls and other duties paid by the merchants. In one such story a house-holder rings a bell and invites the people who were eager to accompany his son on a sea-voyage, without paying the customs duties (*śulka*) or the freight for merchandise (*tarapaṇya*) to bring back goods from foreign countries. In another story, a merchant similarly invites all those who wish to accompany him on a sea-voyage without paying the custom duties, fees payable at military or police stations, or the taxes to be paid for bringing merchandise. Another story also mentions ringing of bells in connection with payment of charges at the military or police stations and the freight for merchandise, and such ringing of bells had as much importance as the alarm for fire, flood, wild animals, thieves and the like.[15]

Aside from trade taxes, another source of revenue was from the city-gates. This was the tax to be paid on goods entering and leaving a town or a city, and amounted to one-fifth of toll dues, which again varied according to the nature of the commodities imported or exported. From the *Sāmantapāsādikā* it is known that *Aśoka*'s income from the four gates of *Pātaliputra* was 400,000 *kahāpaṇ* per day.[16] In the *Mahā-Ummagga Jātaka* also there is mention of revenue earned from the gates of the city. In that story, a king was pleased with the wisdom of a sage in settling issues of dispute regarding a chameleon, and as an expression of his appreciation the king honored him with the 'revenue taken at the four gates' (*catusudvāresusunkamdāpesi*).[17] Such gate-taxes were admitted later by *Kauṭilya* in *Arthaśāstra*,[18] which he regarded as '*dvāradeya*'. From the commentary on the *Vinayapiṭaka* it is known that the kings used to fix the customs-frontier (*śuṅkaghāta*) in hills, bathing places in rivers, and gates of villages for the collection of toll-taxes (*suṅka*). On the basis of this, R.L. Mehta comments, "Various taxes which are termed '*sunikarh*' or '*sunkaṁ*' must have been in vogue in those times, if *Kauṭilya*, a few centuries later, enumerates them minutely."[19]

The fact that there were other taxes prevalent in those days may be inferred from the story of *Ghata-Jātaka*. In this story it is seen that when the ten sons of *Devagabbhā* conquered all India and lived at *Dvārāvati*, they divided the kingdom into ten shares but forgot to pay the share to their only sister *Añjanā*. The youngest brother *Aṁkura* agreed to pay his own share to his sister, and in lien of that he asked his brothers to remit all the taxes payable in their country.[20] This request indicates that there were other taxes to be paid to the state at that time. But the details of such taxes are not found in Buddhist literature.

Apart from the taxes, revenue of the state was also generated from the state-owned properties like forests, waste-lands etc. All unclaimed property, whether lost or stolen, movable or immovable went to the king. There were also systems of milk-money, often called 'love-offering', as a royal prerogative. These were presents to the king from his countrymen on particular occasions like the birth of a prince or the coronation ceremony. In the *Jātakas*, there is the story of *Suruci Jātaka*, where on the occasion of the birth of Prince *Mahā-panāda*, the son of king *Suruci* and his wife *Sumedhā*, all the people of the two countries came and each dropped a coin in the king's courtyard, and soon the coins turned into a heap. Though the king at first did not wish to accept this money, but at the request of his countrymen, he accepted it.[21] Similarly, in the story of the

*Mahājanaka Jātaka*, it is told that on the occasion of the coronation of King *Mahājanaka*, the people of the country presented offerings to the King.[22]

## NOTES

1. Aśokāvadānaṃ, in *Divyāvadānaṃ*, p. 279.
2. Ghoshal U.N., *Contributions to the History of the Hindu Revenue System*, Calcutta: Calcutta University Press, Senate House, 1929, p. 22.
3. Ghoshal U.N., *Ibid*, p. 23.
4. Monier Monier-Williams, *A Sanskrit English Dictionary*, Oxford: Clarendon Press, 1872.
5. Ghoshal U.N., *The Agrarian System in Ancient India*, Calcutta: Calcutta University Press, Senate House, 1930, pp. 25-27.
6. Gupta, K.M., *The Land System in South India*, Lahore: Motilal Banarsi Dass, 1933; Quoted in Mehta, R.L., *Pre-Buddhist India: A Political, Administrative, Economic, Social, and Geographical Survey of Ancient India: Based Mainly on the Jataka Stories*, Bombay: Examiner Press, 1939, p. 143.
7. Mehta, R.L., *Ibid.*, p. 144.
8. Mehta, R.L., *Ibid.*, p. 145.
9. Gaṇḍatindu-Jātaka, in Francis, H. T. (Transl.) and Cowell, E. B. (ed.), *The Jataka*, Vol. V, Cambridge: Cambridge University Press, 1905, p. 56.
10. Mahāsupina-Jātaka, in Chalmers, Robert (Transl.) and Cowell, E.B. (ed.), *The Jataka*, Vol. I, Cambridge: Cambridge University Press, 1895, p. 190.
11. Mehta, R.L., *op. cit.*, p. 146.
12. Barua, B.M., *Asoka and His Inscriptions*, Part I, Calcutta: New Age Publishers, 1968, p.165.
13. *Digha Nikaya*, Vol. I, p.53; *Dialogues of Buddha*, Vol. I, p.77, quoted in Chakravarti, Uma, *Social Dimensions of Early Buddhism*, New Delhi: Munshiram Manoharlal, 1996, p.70.
14. Mahābodhi Jātaka, in Francis, H.T. (Transl.) and Cowell, E.B. (ed.), *The Jataka*, Vol. V, Cambridge: Cambridge University Press, 1905, p.125.
15. Ghoshal U.N., *Contributions to the History of the Hindu Revenue System*, Calcutta: Calcutta University Press, Senate House, 1929, pp. 88-89.
16. Quoted in Mehta R.L., *Pre-Buddhist India*, p. 147.
17. Mahā-Ummagga Jātaka, in Cowell, E.B. and Rouse, W.H.D. (Trans.), and Cowell, E.B. (ed.) , *The Jātaka*, Vol.VI, Cambridge: Cambridge University Press, 1907, p.173.
18. *Arthashastra*, Vol. II, pp. 6, 21, 22.
19. Mehta, R.L., *op. cit.*, p.147.

20. Ghata-Jātaka, in Rouse, W.H.D. (Trans.) and Cowell, E. B. (ed.) , *The Jātaka*, Vol. IV, Cambridge: Cambridge University Press, 1901, p. 53.
21. Suruci-Jātaka, in Rouse, W.H.D. (Trans.) and Cowell, E.B. (ed.) , *The Jātaka*, Vol. IV, Cambridge: Cambridge University Press, 1901, p. 203.
22. Mahājanaka-Jātaka, in Cowell, E.B. and Rouse, W. H. D. (Trans.), and Cowell, E.B. (ed.) , *The Jātaka*, Vol.VI, Cambridge: Cambridge University Press, 1907, p. 28.

# 7

# Pali and Buddhist Studies: Calcutta University and Some Other institutions of India: A Brief Survey

*Bela Bhattacharya*

*Palibhasa* or Pali Language is comparatively a modern coinage. It is doubtful whether the term Pali for the language was coined by the European Orientalists or the *theras* of Ceylon. But it is certain that it was not before the sixth or seventh century A.D. that the nomenclature Pali came into use for the language of canonical texts of the Theravada Buddhists. However, the term Pali did not occur in any text of *Tipitaka*. It was first used by Buddhaghosa in his *Visuddhimagga* with Pali commentaries and later on the Ceylonese chronicle *Culavamsa* mentioned the term Pali in the sense of original texts of the *Tipitaka*, synonymous with *Buddhavacana, Tanti and Pariyatti*.

Gautama Buddha preached his philosophy, doctrine and discipline for long forty-five years in different *janapadas*—Kasi, Kosala, Anga,

Magadha, Kuru, Pancala, Gandhara etc., where he delivered discourses to the people. After the Buddha's *Parinibbana* his disciples collected the Buddha's sayings, which were collectively called *Buddhavacana*, i.e., the words of the Buddha. In the early period the entire *Buddhavacana* were classified into nine types as *Angas* or limbs, (*Navanga Satthusasana*) namely, (i) *Sutta*—prose sermons, (ii) *Geyya*—sermons in a mixture of prose and verse, (iii) *Veyyakarana* (*Vykarana*)—explanations, commentaries, (iv) *Gatha*—stanzas, (v) *Udana*—pithy sayings, (vi) *Itivuttaka*—short speeches beginning with the words: "Thus spoke the Buddha", (vii) *Jätaka*—stories of former births of Buddha, (viii) *Abbhutadhamma*—reports of miracles, and (ix) *Vedalla*—teachings in the form of questions and answers. This division does not allude to a canon complete in itself, or to definite books, but it was only meant to classify the various types of Buddhist texts according to their form and contents.[1]

"The list of the *Angas* is evidence of the fact that, at the time when the Canon was compiled in its present form, all these diverse forms of Buddhist literature were already in existence. Moreover, there are other passages of the Canon which show us that there was at that time a great mass of short texts, rules of the order, speeches, dialogues, aphorisms in verse, and even minor collections of texts, which passed as "the word of Buddha" (*Buddhavacanam*), and were memorised and recited by the monks. They were recited as a kind of recitative, as all sorts of sacred texts are still recited to this day in India and Ceylon. Among the monks there were *Suttantikas*, reciters of the *Suttantas*, *Dhammakathikas*, preachers of the doctrine and *Vinayadharas*, experts in the discipline".[2]

The *Buddhavacana* was further classified into *Dhamna* and *Vinaya* (doctrine and discipline), and thereafter into three *pitaka*s, i.e. *Tipitaka* namely, *Vinaya*, *Sutta* and *Abhidhamma*. Now the question may arise about the language of *Buddhavancana* or the medium of instruction through which Buddha delivered his discourses to the people of different localities. There is a passage in *Vinaya Cullavagga* (Chapter V) which somewhat enlightens us on this matter. It is stated in *Vinaya Cullavagga* that two *bhikkhus* Yamelu and Tekula approached Buddha and reported that the *bhikkhus* of the *Sangha*, consisting of members coming from different cultural groups, different families and different regions, were polluting the Buddha's doctrine and discipline by promulgating them through *Sakaya Nirutti*, i.e. their own local dialects. The *bhikkhus* requested the Buddha to allow them to translate *Buddhavacana* into *Chandasa*. In response, the Buddha rebuked them and ordered that the *bhikkhus* should rather learn *Sakaya Nirutti* (*Sakaya Niruttiya Buddhavacanamaropetabbam*) and promulgate through it, instead of translating *Buddhavacana* into *Chandasa*. Buddhaghosa meant the term *Chandasa* as Sanskrit (*Sakkata*). As the term *Sanskrita* came later than the period of the Buddha it is presumed that by the term *Chandasa* Buddhaghosa meant Vedic diction or language. Buddhaghosa also explained the term *Sakaya Nirutti* as the language of the Magadha (*Magadhaka Vohara*).

The *theras* of Ceylon also hold the view that the medium of instruction of *Buddhavacana* was called *Magadhi Nirutti* i.e. the language of Magadha. The disciples of the Buddha, who used to discuss the Buddha's teachings and words that later developed into *Buddhavacana*, and kept them in memory were called *Dhammakathika, Matikadhara, Vinayadhara, Suttadhara* etc. Thus, the text of *Tipitaka* compiled that way was also called by Buddhaghosa as Pali i.e. the original texts of the Canon and the Ceylonese monks distinguished them from commentaries (*Palimattam idhanitam naatthi athaakathaidha*). The transition of the nomenclature Pali as original texts to Pali as a language is a natural process. The name Pali occupied the place of *Buddhavacana* and its general characteristics proved that it belonged to the Middle Indo-Aryan language that preserved the words of the Buddha as well as their interpretations. In fact, it is the only ancient Indian language in which the teachings of the Buddha are preserved in original till today. Unfortunately, the tradition of learning the Pali language and literature could not continue in the land of its origin except in some areas of North-East India. We should be grateful to Ven. Anagarika Dhammapala, the founder of the Mahabodhi Society of India, Sir Asutosh Mukerjee, Dr. Dharmanand Kosambi, Ven. Bhikkhu Jagadish Kashyapa, Ven. Rahul Sankrityayan, Ambedkar and also a number of Western scholars, who made great effort to revive the Pali Studies in the land of its origin after a long gap of several centuries. The wave spread through the continents of Europe, Asia and America. In the West, the Buddhist and Pali studies were brought to light by T.W. Rhys Davids, who established the Pali Text Society at London in 1881, besides M. Winternitz, E. Burnouf, Hermann, Olderberg, Sylvain Levi, Louis de La Vallee Poussin, Shcherbatskoi, Emile Senart, Max Wallessar, J.H. Woods, Warren and others.

In the East, the veterans who paved the way for proper learning and research on the subject were Jiun Sonja, Bunyiu Nanjio, J. Takakusu, H. Ui, E. Kanakura, T. Kimura, S. Miyamoto, S. Hanayama, M. Nagai, Urrai Waghihora, Chizene Akanuma. Amongst the Indian scholars Rajendra Lal Mitra, Hara Prasad Shastri, Dharmanand Kosambi, Sharat Chandra Das, Satish Chandra Vidyabhusan, Beni Madhab Barua, Nalinaksha Dutt and C.V. Rajvade.

During the 1950s, as a mark of tribute to the ongoing 2500$^{th}$ year of the Buddha's *Parinirvana*, the Govt. of India introduced a full-fledged and independent department in the Delhi University in 1957 for Buddhist Studies under the leadership of an eminent scholar like Prof. P.V. Bapat.

This paper would make an attempt to present a brief survey of the Pali Studies in India after the 19$^{th}$ century.

## The University of Calcutta

The University of Calcutta, very recently, observed its 150$^{th}$ anniversary and 100$^{th}$ year of the Post Graduate teaching in this University. In this context it would be justified to look back a little when the Department of Pali got the final nod to come into existence in the University. The reasons spelt out by the learned University authorities, while introducing the Department of Pali in the University for the Studies in the Buddhist Literature, were instrumental in establishing the Pali Department. It was said that the objective of the University in undertaking the venture was to open out an opportunity to its advanced students for a comprehensive study of that distinct and wide spread civilisation which was represented by Buddhism. "The fact should not be lost sight of that from the 5$^{th}$ Century to the 12$^{th}$ century AD. Buddhism moulded thoughts ideals and literatures of the entire Far East. The history of Buddhism is also a story of cultural contacts between different groups of people in South, South-East and East-Asia." The Department of Pali Studies was intended to provide opportunities for studying the cultural contacts between all these different regions.

It may also be remembered here that the University of Calcutta has been the pioneer in the field of Pali studies in this part of the country. The students started availing this opportunity since the academic session of 1880-1881 of this university. This university can take pride in its being the first university of India to provide the facilities to the students opting for learning Pali as one of their subjects in school and college level. This trend was clearly observed amongst the students of Rangoon (Myanmar). The jurisdiction of the University of Calcutta during the then British regime was from British Burma to Punjab in the Northern India. In compliance with the request from the Director of Public Instructions, Burmah, the University took up the following resolutions in 1880-81, which are recorded as follows: 'Read a letter from the Director of Public

Instruction, British Burmah, requesting that the necessary arrangements may be made for examining candidates for the BA Examination at Rangoon in the coming November, and that one of the candidates may be allowed to take up Pali as a second language.

*Ordered*

1. That Rangoon be added to the list of Centres for the F.A. Examination.
2. That Pali be added to the list of second language for the Entrance, F.A. and B.A. Examinations.
3. That Dr. Forchammer be requested to set papers for the ensuing F.A. Examination in the Dhammapada and Buddhavamsa, the text books recommended for the examination by the Director of Public Instruction, British Burmah-Minutes for 1879-80, p. 42.

Item No. III (Minutes 1880-81, p. 65, 22nd Jan. 1881) 'Read a letter from the Director of Public Instruction, British Burmah, recommending the following text-books in Pali for the University Examinations, in place of those formerly sanctioned.

For the Entrance Examination

1. Pali Miscellany, by Prof. Trenckner (28 pages of the text);
2. Selections from the Jatakas (Fausboll's edition) the Apannaka Jataka (36 pages of the text);

For the F.A. Examination

1. Jatakas (Fausboll's edition): Vaggo I-IV, inclusive, pp. 95-234.
2. Dhammapada (Fausboll's edition): the First Bhanavaram, pp. 1-35.

For B.A. Examination

1. Kaccayana (Senate's edition);
2. Abhidhammatthasahngaha'

As per resolution, the above text books were accepted and *Abhidhammatthasangaha* had to be printed in Calcutta. These records testify to the facts that Burma, the land of Theravada Buddhism played a significant role in introducing Pali for the first time in the University of Calcutta. As a result, the subject was found to be popular amongst the students of Calcutta and Chittagong apart from Burma. Several schools and colleges in these places were affiliated to all the undergraduate courses in Pali. Although arrangements were made to conduct Pali Honours examination, but no student appeared in it or found a place in the list of Honours graduates in Pali till 1908.

Mr. Mahima Rajan Barua of Presidency College was the first Honours graduate in Pali. It is, however, to be noted that no provision existed in any of the affiliated first grade colleges for a systematic teaching of Pali up to the M.A. standard. It is rather amusing to recall in this connection that Mr. Satish Chandra Acharya, the Principal of Sanskrit College wanted to appear as an examinee for the M.A. Examination of 1901 in Pali, but the authorities found it difficult to get an examiner. They were relieved when Prof. T.W. Rhys Davids expressed his willingness to perform as a question setter and examiner for all the six papers. The same problem cropped up when Mr. Harinath Dey, an eminent scholar, whose fame spread far and wide, offered himself as a candidate for the M.A. examination of 1906 in Pali and once again Mr. Davids came to the rescue of the University. Mr. Dey came out with flying colours having taken the First class First position in the M.A. (Pali) examination. It may also be added here that in 1901 as well as in 1908 and 1909, the examinees of the M.A. (Pali) examinations appeared either as private candidates or non-collegiate candidates.

In appreciation of the need, Late Sir Ashutosh Mukherjee, the then Vice-Chancellor of the University of Calcutta (1906-1914) instructed to make necessary arrangements for introducing Pali and Sanskrit at the Post Graduate level. Thus, teaching of Pali and Sanskrit started in 1907 at the Post Graduate level. Mr. Dharmananda Kosambi, an eminent Maharashtrian scholar was appointed the first lecturer in Pali of the University in 1907.After then Mahamohopadhyay Satish Chandra Vidyabhusan, the Principal of Sanskrit College succeeded Mr. Kosambi as the Pali lecturer to teach Pali in Post-Graduate level. From 1912 onwards the students attended regular classes, appeared in the examinations and became post graduate in Pali. Pali continued to be taught at the Post graduate level in this manner until 1917 when a full-fledged department was made for Pali Studies. The teaching staff consisted of learned persons like Dr. Satish Chandra Vidyabhusan, Mr. D.R. Bhandarkar, Babu Surendra Nath Majumdar and Dr. B.M. Barua, a brilliant scholar and the first Asian to be admitted to the degree of Doctor of Literature in the University of London, was appointed as a University Lecturer. "The Executive Committee recommends that Dr. Benimadhab Barua be appointed in the special grade Rs. 500-25-700 with effect from 1st June 1925, and that he be placed in charge of the Department with the designation of the University Professor as a personal distinction."

Apart from those mentioned above, there were a number of other teachers namely, Babu Nalinaksha Dutt, Bhikshu Kukulnape Devarakshita, Raj guru Bhagabanchandra Mahasthavir, Babu Sailendranath Mitra. Samana Punnananda, Samana Rambukwelle Siddhartha, Babu Gakuldas Dey. The services of some teachers belonging to other Departments like History and Sanskrit were also required to teach special papers in Pali.

Dr. Ramesh Chandra Majumdar was appointed to deliver lectures on Geography of Ancient India to the students of Pali and Sanskrit.

As a result of appointments of these eminent scholars and learned Buddhist bhikkhus, there was a wonderful union of experts on the Western and traditional methods. Mr. Suniti Kumar Chatterjee, the erudite scholar, joined the Pali Department, whose honorary services were requisitioned to teach Pali and Philology (1925-26). With the sudden demise of Dr. Satish Chandra Vidyabhusan, who functioned so successfully since the beginning of the Post Graduate studies in Pali, a vacuum was created in the Department. At this juncture Dr. B.M. Barua, the well-known scholar took up the responsibility as the in-charge of the Department and carried out the affairs of Pali Department with great reputation (1925-1948). In 1927, Dr. Nalinaksha Dutt, another stalwart in Buddhism joined the Department. During this intervening period great scholars like Dr. Hemchandra Roy Choudhury, Dr. Prabodhchandra Bagchi, Dr. Benoy Chandra Sen and Nalininath Dasgupta from the Department of Ancient Indian History and Culture, as well as learned scholars like Dr. Satkari Mukherjee from the Sanskrit Department joined the Department of Pali.

It is worthwhile to remember here that the services of eminent scholars from the Pali Department were also requisitioned by other Departments. For example, Dr. B.M. Barua taught in the Department of Ancient Indian History and Culture for about thirty long years as honorary lecturer on Buddhism and Jainism. Sri Gukul Das Dey shouldered the task of teaching Pali in the Department of Indian vernaculars and after his retirement Sri Dwijendralal Barua was assigned the job of teaching Pali in the Department of Modern Indian languages. Incidentally, the revised syllabus for MA Examinations as introduced by Dr. Barua, referred above, came into effect from the year 1955 during the time of Dr. N. Dutt.

On the retirement of Dr. N. Dutta in 1958, Dr. Anukul Chandra Banerjee was appointed to the Chair and continued till 1975. During his tenure, the number of both teaching staff and students went up appreciably. Amidst other charges in the teaching personnel, Rev. Dharmadhar Mahasthavir, the Tripitaka Visarad and Principal of Nalanda Vidyabhavan, a famed oriental scholar, was appointed as an honorary part-time lecturer in 1966 to teach *Abhidhamma* in the post-graduate classes. Dr. Asha Das served in the same manner and was entrusted with the teaching of Pali in the Department of Modern Indian Languages. Dr. Shyam Sundar Banerjee was appointed in the newly created post of part-time lecturer with remuneration. The vacant post of full-time lecturer was filled up with the appointment of Dr. Dipak Kumar Barua who served the Rabindra Bharati University in various capacities.

The upward trend in the numerical strength of students continued all these years. Dr. Kanailal Hazra, on return from Ceylon, resumed teaching as a full time lecturer of the newly introduced subject "Asian Buddhism". The Department of Pali had to suffer an irreparable loss with the death of Mr. P.C. Majumdar who dedicated his life to the cause of promotion of Pali Studies. Following the retirement of Prof. A.C. Banerjee in 1975, the onus of conducting the affairs of the Department of Pali fell on Dr. Sukumar Sengupta. After Dr. Sengupta, Dr. Dipak Kumar Barua took over the headship of the Department as a Reader. In 1978, Dr. Barua was appointed as a Professor, the post remaining vacant for a long time since the retirement of Dr. A.C. Banerjee.

Dr. Barua, on assuming the post, brought about remarkable changes in the affairs of the Department. Rev. Dharmapal Bhikkhu, Dr. Binayendranath Choudhary and Dr. Sukomal Choudhury were appointed as part time lecturers. Dr. Asha Das took over as full time lecturer. Dr. Barua took the initiative to introduce Certificate and Diploma Courses in Pali Language and Literature and this came into effect during the session of 1980-81. With Dr. Barua in the Chair and Dr. Kanailal Hazra as Head of the Department, some vacant posts were duly filled up. Dr. Asha Das was elevated to the post of Reader,

Dr. Bela Bhattacharya was appointed as a lecturer, and the services of Dr. Mrinal Kanti Ganguly belonging to the Sanskrit and Dr. Kshanika Saha to the Ancient Indian History and Culture were requisitioned by Dr. Hazra.

The University introduced Pre-M.A. Course catering to the needs of the Graduates to be eligible for admission to the M.A. Course. The arrangements for holding Pre-M.A. classes were made for the first time in the Department, with effect from September 1984 owing to the initiative and effective steps taken by Dr. Asha Das in seeking permission from the University authorities to open the Pre-M.A. classes in Pali for the benefit of the students. In 1983, M.Phil Course was introduced in the Department. Till 2006, approximately 50 dissertations were submitted under the guidance of the teachers of the Department of Pali.

With the creation of the Department of Pali in the University of Calcutta, the teaching staff tirelessly pursued their research works in various fields of Buddhist Studies—epigraphy, art and archeology etc. related to Buddhism. As a result of their researches many more aspects of Buddhism have been highlighted and much light has been thrown on these matters. The following references would be suffice to bear testimony to the fact that as a result of these researches, significant progress has been made to augment our knowledge about Buddhism and the Indian Culture. Only a partial list is given below:

*A History of the Pre-Buddhistic Indian Philosophy* by Prof. B.M. Barua, Published in 1921 from the Calcutta University.

*Aspects of the Mahayana Buddhism and its relations to Hinayana* by Prof. Nalinaksha Dutt, published in 1930.

*Sarvastivada Literature* by Prof. Anukul Chandra Banerjee, published in 1957. It should be mentioned here that he also guided about 20 students in their research for Ph.D. Degree.

*Banglay Bauddhadharma* (in Bengali) by Sri Nalininath Dasgupta, published in 1948.

*Significance and importance of Jatakas* and *Democracy in the Early Buddhist Sangha* by Gokuldas De published in 1951 and 1955 respectively.

*Buddhist Centres in Ancient India* by Prof. Binayendranath Choudhury, the first Ph.D. student under Prof. A.C. Banerjee, published in 1969.

*Bangla Sahitye Bauddha Dharma O Sanskriti* (in Bengali) Research work by Dr. Asha Das, the first lady student in the Department of Pali to be awarded D. Phil Degree in 1966 under the supervision of Prof. A.C. Banerjee.

*An Analytical Study of the Four Nikayas* by Prof. Dipak Kumar Barua, published in 1971.

*Buddhism in South-east Asia*: *Mainly Based on Epigraphic Sources*, by Dr. Sukumar Sengupta, published in 1994.

*History of Theravada Buddhism in South-East Asia* by Dr. Kanailal Hazra, published in 1982.

*Analytical Study of the Abhidharmakosa* by Prof. Sukomal Chaudhuri, published in 1976.

*Facets of Early Buddhism: A Study of Fundamental Principles* by Prof. Bela Bhattacharya, published in 1995.

There are many other research publications by the Department of Pali, Calcutta University. In addition to research publications, several other contributions have been made in the form of articles etc. In this connection, mention may be made of certain other works which have earned appreciation from those interested in Buddhism and Pali literature. They are as follows:

1. *Journal of the Department of Pali*, University of Calcutta, I-XV volumes (1982 to 2007)
2. *Bauddhakosa*, (Encyclopaedia in Bengali), Vol. I-VI (1985-86 to 2004-2007).
3. *Haraprasad Smarane*, a special volume, 2007.

## Courses

The Department of Pali of the University of Calcutta offers the following courses:

- One year Pre M.A.
- Two years M.A.
- Two years M.Phil
- One year Certificate in Pali Language
- One year Diploma in Pali Langauge
- One year Certificate in Tibetan Language
- One year Diploma in Tibetan Language
- U.G. Diploma in Buddhist Studies—Self Finance
- M.A. Buddhist Studies—Self Finance
- Ph.D. Programme

Two years M.A. Course in Pali is conducted through Four Semester System, and duration of each Semester is 6 (Six) months.

The First Semester covers:

- Select Pali Canonical Texts (Vinaya Pitaka) viz. (i) Bhikkhu Patimokkha (Pali), (ii) Mahavagga: Chapters (Khandhalas) I and II, and (iii) Cullavagga Chapters IV and VI.
- History of Buddhism and Buddhist Literature—Pali, Sanskrit, Buddhist Sanskrit
- Pali, Sanskrit and Prakrit grammar.
- History of Prakrit languages.
- Classification of Language, the Indo-Aryan Family of Languages, Development of Sound-System, Comparative difference, Asokan Dialects, Origin, Development and History of Pali Language.

The followings are taught in the Second Semester:

- Select Pali Canonical texts (Suttapitaka) and Select Later Pali and Buddhist Sanskrit texts that include: Dighanikaya:

Brahmajala Sutta; Majjhimanikaya – Aryapariyesana Sutta, Dhammapada: Yamakavagga, Cittavagga, Maggavagga and Bhikkhuvagga, Suttanipata: Khaggavisana Sutta and Munisutta,Theragatha: Anuruddha Thera, Therigatha: Kisagotami.

- Select Later Pali and Buddhist Sanskrit texts comprising Milindapanha (Sasanavamsa Chapter III (Portion relating to Subannbhumi); Lalitavistara: Chapter X (Lipimalasandarsanaparivarta); Divyavadana: Chapter on Asokavadana.
- Select Pali Abhidharma Texts—Abhidhammattha Sangaha Chapters I, II and VI; Atthasalini (PTS) Introduction (pp. 1-31); Patthana: Uddesa and Niddesa
- Select Sanskrit Philosophical Texts—Abhidharmakosa: Chapter 1; Madhyamikakarika: Chapter I; Nyayabindu: Chapter 1.

The topics that are covered in the Third Semester are as follows:

- Political History, History with Special reference to Original Texts.
- Religious History—Life of Buddha; Early Monastic Buddhism; Facts of early Buddhism; Royal Patronage; Decadence of Buddhism.
- Early Budhhist Literature and Philosophy comprising of Special Canonical Texts—Samyutta Nikaya Texts; Anguttara Nikaya: Ananda Vagga; Udana: Jacchanda Vagga; Jataka (ed. Fousboll): Ghata Jaytaka (454) Dasaratha Jataka (461), Mahabodhi Jataka (528) and MahajanakaJataka (No. 539).
- Special non-canonical texts—Milindapanha (ed Trenckner) Mendakapanha pp. 188-234; Telakatahagatha (PTS), 1884); Vimanavatthu Serissakavatthu
- Mahayana Literature and Philosophy—Select Mahayana and Tantrayana texts
- Suvarnaprabhasa Sutra—Chapter XIX; Saddharmapundarika Sutra—Chapters II–III.

- Buddhacarita—Chapters I-III; Bodhicaryavatara—Chapters I-III; Prajnapayavinscayasiddhi (G.O.S.)—Chapters I-III.
- Epigraphy, Iconography, Art and Architecture, Select Prakrit and Sanskrit Inscriptions with Paleography.
- Inscriptions of Asoka; Piprahwa Vase Inscriptions; Mahasthan Stone Plaque Inscription; Bharhut Buddhist Pillar Inscription of the time of the Sungas; Wardak Vase Inscription; Besnagar Column Inscription of Heliodoros; Hathigumpha Inscription of Kharavela; Sui Vihara Inscription; Ara Inscription; Nagarjunikonda Inscription; Nasik Cave Inscription of Vasisthiputra Pulumavi; Allahabad Pillar Inscription of Samudragupta; Sanchi Stone Inscription of Chandragupta II; Bhitari Pillar Inscription of Skandagupta; Banskhera Grant of Harsa; Khalimpur Inscription of Dharmapaladeva; Nalanda Copper Plate of Devapaladeva; Rampal Copper plate of Sri Chandra; Deopara Inscription of Vijaysena.
- Asian Buddhism.
- Comparative Study of Buddhist Literature in and outside India—Buddhist Literature in Central Asia; Buddhist Literature in Sri Lanka and Myanmar.

The Fourth Semester syllabus includes:

- Vibhanga—Paceayakara Vibhanga (with commentary); Kathavatthu—Pathamavagga.
- Dhammasangani (PTS ed.) pp. 1-75; Visuddhimagga Pannabhuminiddesa; Nettippakarana: The Sixteen Haras and Five Nayas.
- Select Madhyainika, Yogacara and Old Bengali texts bearing on Buddhism—Madhayamikakarika, Chapter XXIV and XXV; Lankavatara Sutra, Chapter II.
- Astasahasrika Prajnaparamita, Chapter I-IV; Vijnaptimatrataasiddhi Vimsika (Krikas only); Caryapada Nos. 5, 6, 8, 10, 14, 17, 20, 28, 32 and 40.

- Buddhist Art and Iconography.
- Buddhist and Allied Culture in Tibet, Central Asia, China, Japan. Indo-China and Indonesia.
- Comparative Study of Allied Indian Literature.
- Comparative Study of allied Indian Religious and Philosophical System: Buddhist, Jaina, Sankhya and Vedanta.
- Special Buddhist Historical Records, Archaeological Reports and Ancient Indian Geography.
- Historical and Topographical Information relating to Bihar: Rajagriha, Nalanda, Vikramsila, Bodhgaya; Orissa: Ratnagni; West Bengal: Karnasuvarna, Jagjivanpur; Bangladesh: Paharpur, Mainamati; Uttar Pradesh: Sarnath, Kusinara; Madhya Pradesh: Sanchi, Bharhut; Nepal: Kapilavastu; Pakistan Taxila.
- Ancient Indian Geography.
- Buddhism and Allied Culture in Burma, Siam and Ceylon.

The reputation of teaching and research aspires the foreign students to get admission to the Pali Department for studying Pali and Buddhism. The students from Thailand, Myanmar, Vietnam, Ceylon, South Korea, Japan, and Bangladesh come to study in M.A. and Ph.D. Research Projects. Recently the Undergraduate Diploma in Buddhist Studies and M.A. Course in Buddhist Studies have been introduced under the self finance schemes. Thus, appreciable progress seems to have been achieved by the Department of Pali in the University of Calcutta to enrich the knowledge of Buddhism and Pali and further headway in this connection is sure to be made in the days to come.

## Jadavpur University

Center for Buddhist Studies, sponsored by the ICPR, New Delhi has been introduced in the Department of Philosophy, Jadavpur University in 2013 to promote Buddhist Philosophical Studies.

## The Asiatic Society, Kolkata

The Society, established in 1784 in Kolkata by Sir William Jones, is a rich repository of vast and invaluable treasure of rare manuscripts and other source materials on the history of India and Buddhism.

## Sanskrit College, Kolkata

The Sanskrit College is under the jurisdiction of Calcutta University and caters to the teaching of Pali up to the Honours Graduate standard. In bygone days many Pali teaching staff from Presidency College used to take classes here. Since its inception the College has sailed successfully toward its hallowed goal of preparing students for further higher studies and research work.

## Visva Bharati, Shantiniketan (West Bengal)

The origin of the University dates back to 1863, when Maharshi Debendranath Tagore, the zamindar of Silaidaha in East Bengal, set up an ashram on the tract of land given to him by Babu Sitikanta Sinha, the zamindar of Raipur, a neighbouring village not far from Bolepur and present-day Santiniketan. In the present day Visva Bharati is a Central University for research and teaching in India, located in the twin towns of Santiniketan and Sriniketan in the State of West Bengal. It was founded by Rabindranath Tagore who named it Visva Bharati, which means the communion of the world with India. In its initial years Tagore expressed his dissatisfaction with the word 'university', since university is translated into Vishva-Vidyalaya, which is smaller in scope than Visva Bharati. Until independence it was a college. Soon after independence, in 1951, the institution was given the status of a university and was renamed Visva Bharati University. The University offers courses in major languages that include:

- Sanskrit
- Pali
- Prakrit
- Indo-Tibetan Studies
- Chinese

The courses related to Buddhism run by the University are as follows:

- Preparatory Course—Indo-Tibetan Studies

This One Year Preparatory Course is conducted for the students without knowledge of Tibetan in reading and writing to train them in basic Tibetan, colloquial and Buddhist Terminology, introduce them to the general outlines of Buddhist thought and the specifics of Tibetan Culture and Civilization.

- B.A. (Hons.) Course—Indo-Tibetan Studies

Three Years course consisting of eight examination papers of four hours duration carrying 100 marks each, of which 20 is awarded by internal assessment.

- M.A. Course—Indo-Tibetan Studies

Eight papers carrying 40 marks each plus 10 marks reserved for internal assessment.

Other courses offered by the University are:

- Certificate—Indo Tibetan Studies—2 years
- Diploma—Indo Tibetan Studies—1 year
- Foreign Casual Course—1 year

The Centre for Buddhist Studies of the University plays a significant role in promoting and understanding different aspects of Buddhism.

## Ram Thakur College, Agartala, Tripura

This is the only college outside Calcutta, founded in 1967, facilitates the student of vast area of the North-East region to learn Pali Language and to have more in-depth knowledge about Buddhism. Now it runs a course for the graduate level and efforts are on to extend up to the upper-level of studies as the student strength may demand so.

The other institutes which offer courses on Buddhism/Pali/Prakrit or associated with the activities related to Buddhism/Pali/Prakrit are as follows:

- **Jagadguru Ramanandacharya Rajasthan Sanskrit University, Jaipur**.
- **The Centre for Buddhist Studies, University of Sukhadia, Udaipur** under Dr. Rajnish Shukla.
- **Veer Kunwar Singh University, Arrah, Bihar**— Departments Pali, Prakrit and Buddhist Studies.
- **Mithila Research Institute, Darbhanga**. One of the known publications of this Institute is *Buddhism in Mithila* by Prof. Vijay Thakur.
- **Lucknow University**, Pali is taught in the Department of Sanskrit.
- **Kendriya Sanskrit Vidyapeethas** of Lucknow, and Allahabad and all other Kendriya Sanskrit Vidyapeethas.
- **Aligarh Muslim University** was established in 1920, and the Department of Sanskrit started in the same year. At that time, Acharya Pandit Ramswarup Shastri was the Head of the Department of Sanskrit. At present Sanskrit Pali is taught in the Department of Sanskrit and Prof. Satya Prakash Sharma of this department is an authority on Sanskrita Pali. Professor Satyadev Kausik is the Chairman in the Department of Sanskrit as a Professor of Pali since 2000.

- **Bundelkhand University of Jhansi** has introduced the self finance course in Buddhist Studies.
- **Centre for Buddhist Studies, Mahatma Gandhi International Hindi University, Wardha, Maharashtra** offrers:
  - Two Years Full Time MA in Buddhist Studies.
  - One Year Part Time P.G. Diploma in Pall Languages and Literature (since 2010).
  - P.G. Diploma in Buddhist Studies (since 2010).
  - P.G. Diploma Tibetan Language (since 2004).
  - P.G. Diploma in Tibetan Buddhism (since 2004).
  - P.G. Diploma in Buddhist Tourism and Guiding (since 2011).

## Nava Nalanda Mahavihara

Dr. Rajendra Prasad, the first President of India, announced an institution would be opened at Nalanda for Pali Studies. In 1951, the Magadh Institute of Post Graduate Studies and Research in Pali and Allied Languages and Buddhist Learning was established. In 1956, the Govt. of Bihar regularised the Nava Nalanda Mahavihira, with Bhikshu Jagdish Kashyap as its Founder Director. Since then the Mahavihara is engaged with the objective of promoting advance studies in Pali and Buddhist learning and publishing works in this discipline. One of the significant works of the Mahavihara has been the publication of the entire Pali Tipitaka (41 volumes), with Atthakathas (commentaries) on the Pali Tipitaka, Tikas and Anutikas on them and other Pali texts, in Devanagari script, under the General Editorship of Ven. Bhikshu Jagdish Kashyap. The complete 41 volumes set of the Devanagari Tipitaka totaling has become very popular.

The Mahavihara is imparting education in the following subjects:

- Pali and Early Buddhism

- Buddhist Philosophy (both Hinayana & Mahayana)
- Logic and Epistemology including outlines of the Indian Philosophy and Comparative Religion.
- Ancient Indian and Asian Studies with special reference to the Buddhist History and Culture and spread of Buddhism.
- Linguistics and Modern Indian Languages
- Tibetan and Chinese Studies including Mongolian, Korean and Japanese Language.

Nava Nalanda Mahavihara has also brought out a few Research volumes. The first two volumes done under the able and meticulous editorship of Dr. Satkari Mookerji caught the attention of the great Buddhist scholars, particularly of Japan.

Pali-Hindi Sabdakosha, Vols. I and II, edited by Rabindra Panth, the Director of Nava Nalanda, Mahavihara have been published with the help of some Pali scholars.

The establishment of Nava Nalanda Mahavihara, which is popularly known as Pali Institute has been playing a great role in making Pali popular. The students, particularly the monk students from Myanmar, Sri Lanka, Thailand, Cambodia, Vietnam, Japan and Tibet come here regularly to study Pali and the Buddhist teachings. Slowly but steadily the local people in particular and others in general have been coming here to know about the Buddha and his teachings, as well as Pali language in which he gave his teachings. They also come here to know about the spread of Buddhism in the world.

The Mahavihara conducts the following courses. The Syllabus for each of the courses is prepared by a Group of Scholars of the respective subjects:

- Certificate in Pali
- Diploma in Japanese (2 Years)
- Diploma in Tibetan (2 Years)
- Diploma in Chinese (2 Years)

- Diploma in Sanskrit (2 Years)
- Diploma in Hindi (2 Years)

For Pali Acharya Course the Nava Nalanda Mahavihara is affiliated to the Kameshwar Singh Sanskrit University, Darbhanga.

## Delhi University

In the year 1957, the University introduced Buddhist Studies as a full-fledged academic discipline under the leadership of P.V. Bapat. The Department initially began with research activities such as M.Lit. and Ph.D. etc. Certificate and Diploma Courses in Pali and Tibetan were added later on. N.H. Samtani was the first awardee of the PhD degree in Buddhist Studies from this department. In 1979, MA course in Buddhist Studies was introduced. The Department of Buddhist Studies of Delhi University runs the following courses:

- Certificate and Diploma in Tibetan (part time basis)
- M.A. (with various specialization groups like Pali, Sanskrit, Tibetan, Chinese, Japanese, History and Philosophy).
- M.Phil and Ph.D. full time courses.

In addition to the Delhi University, there are about 40 educational institutions including colleges, universities and research institutes in Uttar Pradesh, which run various courses in Buddhist studies either as full-fledged Departments of Buddhist Studies or some specific subjects related to Buddhism such as:

- Pali, Mahayana Buddhism
- Tibetan or Tantrika Buddhism
- Buddhist Philosophy
- Ancient Indian and Asian Studies

*2500 Years of Buddhism* edited by P.V. Bapat, published in the year 1956, is a landmark in the recent history of the Buddhist Studies.

Varanasi and Sarnath are two very important places for Pali/ Buddhist Studies.

There are four universities situated in these two places, namely:

- **Benaras Hindu University (BHU)**
- **The Sampurnanand Sanskrit University**
- **The Mahatma Gandhi Kashi Vidyapeeth**
- **The Central Institute of Higher Tibetan Studies University), Sarnath.**

## Banaras Hindu University (BHU)

Banaras Hindu University has two departments engaged in Pali/ Prakrit/Buddhist Studies:

Department of Pali and Buddhist Studies (Faculty of Arts).
Department of Philosophy and Religion—Jainism and Buddhism.
Department of Sanskrit.

The courses they offer are:

- Undergraduate course in Pali Studies (Department of Pali and Buddhist Studies).
- M.A. and B.A. Courses through semester system.
- Two Years Diploma Course in Pali.

## Sampurnanand Sanskrit University

Sampurnanand Sanskrit University was established in 1958 by Late Jagnnath Upadhyay. There are many Departments but the Department of Pali and Theravada Buddhism runs the courses as follows:

- Shastri (B.A.): Three years course
- Acharya (M.A.): Two years course
- Buddhist Philosophy (M.A.): Two years

- Pali Language, Certificate One year
- Pali Language, Diploma One year
- M.Phil. One year course
- Tibetan course (Tibbeti igama)
- Shastri (B.A.): Three years
- Acharya (M.A.): Two years
- Tibetan Diploma: One year

## The Mahatma Gandhi Kashi Vidyapeeth, Varanasi

- The Department of History of this Vidyapeeth has undertaken the responsibility of Buddhist Studies.

## The Central University of Tibetan Studies

The Central University of Tibetan Studies (Formerly known as Central Institute of Higher Tibetan Studies), Sarnath, Varanasi.

This Central University is dedicated to the Tibetan Buddhism and also provide the facilities to study Pali.

There are many scholars of Buddhism who teach in the above mentioned institutions.

There are two prominent seats of Buddhist Learning in Jammu and Kashmir—Ladakh and Leh. Ladakh is a place where Buddhism is a predominant religious faith. The Gompas spread all over Ladakh have been rich repositories of Tibetan texts, and they impart Buddhist education to its inmates as well as to the common people. Ladakh and Tibet had close contact with each other and therefore the deep impact of Tibetan form of Buddhism and Tibetan culture is quite visible in Ladakh.

In 1959, the Government of India, persuaded by Ven. Kushok Bakula, established the Central Institute of Buddhist Studies at Choglamsar, Leh. The Institute is a Deemed University and provides education from Class VI to Research Level including PhD degree. This Institute is financed by the Ministry of Culture, Govt. of India and internally autonomous as far a administration is concerned. The Institute is affiliated to the Sampurnanand Sanskrit University, Varanasi.

## University of Jammu

The Department of Buddhist Studies, University of Jammu, established in May 1987, offers M.A. and Ph.D. programmes.

The Department excels in:

- Pali and Theravada Buddhism
- Sanskrit and Mahayana Buddhism
- Buddhist Philosophy
- History of Buddhism
- Buddhist Art
- Architecture and Archaeology
- Tibetan Buddhism
- Tantric Buddhism
- Contemporary Buddhism

## Magadh University, Bodhgaya, Bihar

This University, established in 1962, offers Courses in Pali/Buddhist Studies. The Departments engaged in teaching Buddhist philosophy and Buddhism are:

- Department of Ancient India and Asian Studies,
- Department of Pali,
- Department of Buddhist Studies.

Kashi Prasad Jaiswal Research Institute, located in the premises of the Patna Museum, preserves a rich treasure of Buddhist Antiquities, Manuscripts on Mahayana and Tantra texts.

## Nagarjuna University, Andhra Pradesh

Andhra Pradesh has produced a number of leading scholars in the field of Buddhist thought like Acharya Nagarjuna, Aryadeva, Buddhagosa, Dirinaga, Bhavaviveka and Dharmakirti. Andhra is considered to be the cradle of Mahayanism and Vajrayana. This region was responsible for initiating newer developments in the Buddhist creed. Acharya Nagarjuna, the first systematiser of the Madhyamika School of the Mahayana Buddhism, made Andhradesa his home and propagated his philosophy from Sriparvatha Vijayapuri in Guntur District. After Nagarjuna, Aryadeva along with a host of other intellectuals improved the status of the Mahayana. Amaravati and Nagarjuna Konda became famous centres propagating the Mahayana Studies and attracting scholars from different parts of the then civilised world.

The University, being located in a region rich with Buddhist association and cherishing the name of Acharya Nagarjuna, felt that it was its sacred duty to promote in the region the Studies to which Acharya Nagarjuna devoted his life. On March 16, 1982, the Centre for Mahayana Buddhist Studies was inaugurated by the King of Bhutan, His Majesty Jigme Singhe Wangchuk. On May 26, 1983, on the eve of the Buddha Jayanti Day, the Faculty of the Buddhist Studies started functioning with Prof. K. Satchidananda Murthy as its first Honorary Director and Dr. S. Nagaraju as the Reader and Head of the Faculty.

At present, the Head of the Centre is Prof. M.V. Ramkumar Ratnam. Currently four faculty members are working at the Centre, namely Prof. M.V. Ramkumar Ratnam, Prof. J. Seetaramma, Sri. L. Uday Kumar.

Prof. Akira Saito from Tokyo University, Japan, Prof. G.C. Nayak, the Ex Vice-Chancellor from the Shri Jagannath Sanskrit Vishvavidayalaya, Puri, Prof. N.H. Samtani, from the Department of Buddhist Studies, B.H.U., Banaras, and Dr. C.T. Dorji from Bhutan have served this University as Visiting Professors.

Department/Centre for Buddhist Studies, **Himachal Pradesh University, Shimla** is dedicated to research works on Buddhism and offers Diploma Course in Tibetan.

**Guru Gobind Singh Department of Religious Studies of the Punjabi University, Patiala** has a full-fledged unit of Buddhist Studies that offers M.A. Course in Buddhist Studies.

In Dharmashala, Himachal Pradesh, many institutes of Tibetan Buddhism and Culture are run by the Tibetans, but they are not very organized. The scope for development of these institutes is immense.

**Mahadev Desai Samajseva Mahavidyalaya Mahadev Desai College of Social Work, Ahmedabad**, affiliated to Gujarat Vidyapith, offers M.A., M.Phil courses and Ph.D degrees in Buddhism.

**Sikkim Institute of Higher Nyingma Studies**, stores rare manuscripts on Buddhist Literature in Sanskrit and Tibetan.

Maharashtra is highly conscious about preserving the cultural and religious heritage of Buddhism as well as imparting its teaching. Dr. Babasaheb Ambedkar gave a significant boost for the study of Buddhology in this region. Almost all the universities of Maharashtra have the provision of teaching Pali at the Under Graduate and Post Graduate level besides research facilities. Pune in particular and Maharashtra in general had a long chain of eminent Buddihist scholars namely, Dharmanand Kosambi, Rantungar, RV. Bapat. V.V. Gokhale, Bhimrao Ramji Ambedkar etc. who initiated the process of Pali and Buddhist Studies in the state.

**Fergusson College**, Pune was the first college to offer courses in Pali at the PG Level.

**Pune University** has two separate departments:

- Departments for Pali that conducts Course on Buddhist Studies.
- Department of Buddhist Studies and Dr. Ambedkar's Thought.

The Department of Pali and Prakrit Languages of the **Rashtrasant Tukadoji Maharaj Nagpur University** runs graduate as well as post-graduate courses and also undertakes research activities.

**Dr. Ambedkar's Marathwad University, Aurangabad** conducts courses on Buddhism through the Department of Pali and Buddhism and the Centre of Buddhist Studies.

**The Takshashila College under the Amravati University,** Amravati imparts Pali and Prakrit in the Department of Pali and Prakrit.

North Maharsahtra University, Jalgaon provides BA Course in Pali.

**Swami Ramananda Tirthu University**, Nanded provides B.A. course in Pali. Pali is a popular subject in Maharashtra, It is taught at the Higher Secondary Level also.

Pali and the Buddhist Studies are new to the Khandesh region, North Maharashtra. The person who introduced it to the Khandesh region is Annasaheb Vyankatrao Randhir. He established the "**Kisan Vidya Prasarak Education Society**" in 1941, the objective of which was to educate poor boys and girls. Annasaheb several times visited Ven. Bhadant Anand Kausalyayan, who is an eminent personality in the Buddhist world. Annasaheb used to think about the Buddha, Dhamma and Sangha. After studying Buddhism he accepted the path of Buddhism on May 5, 1973.Thereafter, Annasaheb introduced Pali to Kisan Vidya Prasarak Sanstha, as he had assured Anand

Kausalyayan of starting Pali. The second reason was that while studying Buddhism he was much influenced by the Buddhist Literature.

Annasaheb started the subject in his **Kisan Vidya Prasarak Sanstha's Popatlal Dhanjibhai Malaviya College** in the Khandesh region.

Another institution in the Khandesh region—**Vardhini Sabha's Arts, Science and Commerce College** in Dhule was established in 1966 and started courses in Pali to show the path of Lord Buddha to the society.

**The University of Mumbai** provides teaching of Pali up to the Under Graduate Level. **Siddhartha College**, established by Babasaheb Ambedkar, introduced Pali at the Under Graduate level. Later on, this college got recognition from the Mumbai University as its P.G. Centre and Dept. of Buddhist Studies to run the MA and research programme. M.A. in Pali also has been introduced.

**K.J. Somaiya Centre of Buddhist Studies** deserves a special mention in this context. Initially, it had been set up as a research centre, but gradually it started conducting Buddhist Studies.

**The Mahabodhi Society of Kolkata**, which is also the Head Quarter, has published a number of journals and other literature on Buddhism.

**The Mahabodhi Society of Bangalore** has published low price books on Pali and Buddhist Studies under the editorship of its Founder Director Ven. Buddharakkhita.

**Bauddha Dharmankur Sabha (The Bengal Buddhist Association)**, situated at the Buddhist Temple Street, Bowbazar, Kolkata, was established by Ven. Kripasaran Mahasthavira, who was born on June 22, 1865 in Unainpura of Chittagong (now in Bangladesh) in a Barua family. It was Kripasaran who soon emerged as the pole star of modern Buddhism of Bengal. His mother dedicated him to the Buddhist Sangha. After initiation in Theravada Buddhism he was known as Kripasaran Mahathera in 1885 by a renowned Buddhist monk Sudhanchandra Mahasthavira of Unainpura Vihar (Lankaram). A number of books on Buddhism have been published from this renowned Institution.

**Mahabodhi International Meditation Centre at Choglamsar, Leh** was established by Sanghasena, a scholar and practitioner of Theravada Buddhism.

**Vipassana Research Institute, Igatpuri** served the Pali and Buddhist Studies by organising Vipassana Meditation Course for practical experience to general practitioners and scholars.

In modern times, the Vipassana activities started by Acharya Sri S.N. Goenka gave a tremendous fillip to the study of Pali. The meditators, who are a little academically inclined, want to read that literature in which Buddha's teachings in general and his teachings on Vipassana in particular are enshrined. A celebrated exponent of the technique of Vipassana meditation Goenkaji succinctly explains the salient features of the Dhamma taught by the Buddha in the following words: "Dhamma is not a religion. Dhamma is a code of conduct. Dhamma is an ethical, moral way of life. Dhamma is an art of living. Dhamma is to live a happy, healthy, wholesome life. Dhamma is to live peacefully and harmoniously within ourselves and generate a peaceful and harmonious atmosphere around oneself." When he says that Dhamma is not a religion, he means that it is neither a sectarian nor an organized religion, which often does more harm than good. Dhamma taught by the Buddha is scientific and based on universal laws that operate in the moral and spiritual world. He says that the term Dhamma occurs many times in the entire Pali literature consisting of the Tipitakas, Atthakathas Tikas and Anuttikas, but everywhere it means universal laws and not organised religion.

In fact, the term 'Bauddha' (Buddhism, Buddhist) never occurs in the entire corpus of Pali literature.

In a ten-day course, Sri S.N. Goenka recites many *gathas* and passages in Pali from the Tipitaka, explains their meanings and shows how they are relevant to practicing Vipassana. By the time the ten-day course is over, serious meditators develop desire to read Pali themselves and know more about the Buddha's Vipassana technique. Goenkaji's method of acquainting meditators with Pali language and introducing them to the words of the Buddha is brilliant inasmuch as it is practical and result-oriented. People of different professions feel greatly inspired to learn Pali and see for themselves what great spiritual treasure is enshrined there.

The Western meditators, particularly the Americans, take great pains to collect Pali words found in the chanting of Sri S.N. Goenka and they make themselves familiar with them. The Western scholars and meditators are taking keen interest in learning Pali.

When Goenkaji first started teaching the technique of Vipassana, at least some meditators wanted to know from him the *suttas*, in which the technique of Vipassana as taught by the Buddha is described. Of course, he teaches the *Saripatthana Sutta*, word by word in seven-day *Satipaishana* courses, but still the curiosity of a large number of meditators to know more about the Buddha and his teachings, particularly on Vipassana, could not be satisfied by reading a few *suttas* to them and by chanting a few *gathas* from the Dhammapada.

By the time Goenkaji had introduced the technique of Vipassana to a large number of meditators, the Nalanda edition of the Tipitaka in the Devanagri script was exhausted. No copy was available there. So he could not ask the meditators to buy copies of the Tipitaka in the Devanagri script from the market. Vipassanacharya Sri Satyanarayan Goenka resolved to cater for the needs of the meditators by taking upon himself the Himalayan task of publishing the three *Pitakas* along with their *Atthakathas, Tikas* and *Anutikas*. He himself had realised the importance of *pariyatti* (theory) in strengthening *patipatti* (practice). So, for providing Pali books to academically inclined meditators in particular and common readers in general, he established Vipassana Research Institute (VRI) in 1985 to publish the entire set of Pali Literature.

Since VRI was established in 1985 it has come a long way. It has brought out not only one hundred and forty volumes of Pali Tipitaka in Devanagari script for the first time, but also published many books to remove the misconceptions that the people have about the Buddha.

The publication is authentic as it is based on the *Chattha sangayana* edition of Myanmar. This edition has many useful features. In the *Suttasara*, given in the beginning, the contents of the *suttas* are briefly given in Hindi. The second significant feature is that the important words such as *sari, sampajanna* and *vedana* connected with Vipassana are highlighted. The important passages connected with *saniatha* and *vipassana* are also highlighted. An exhaustive word index is given at the end of each book. There are many other Buddhist Meditation centres in India but I am not discussing about them here.

The Department of Buddhist and Tibetan Languages of the **Panjab University, Chandigarh**, which was established in 1882, runs M.A. Course in Buddhist and Tibetan Studies as well as Chinese and Tibetan languages. It has commenced Semester system from the session 2012-2013.

**Bhagwan Buddha University, Bangalore** runs distance courses in Pali and Buddhism which were introduced in 2010.

The following courses are conducted by this University:

- B.A. Honours.
- M.A.

- M.Phil.
- Ph.D.

**Gautama Buddha University, Noida** started functioning from 2008 under the Govt. of U.P. Act, 2002. There are eight schools namely, Art, Humanity, Law, Applied Sciences, Architecture, Buddhist Studies, Biotechnology and Engineering. Buddhist Studies course started from 2012. The GBU runs the following courses:

- M.A. (Two years course).
- M.Phil. (One year course).
- Ph.D.

**Rashtriya Sanskrit Samsthan**, **Deemed University**, which is under the Ministry of Human Resource Development, Government of India offers Prak-Shastri, Shastri and Acharya programmes under Distance Mode of Education. It runs four certificate courses in Pali, Prakrit, Computational Linguistics and Natya Shastra, but it has no other unit beyond Delhi.

Rashtriya Sanskrit Samsthan have a number of campuses, but Pali and Buddhist Studies are conducted in the campuses mentioned below:

- Rashtriya Sanskrit Sansthan,
  Ganganath Jha Campus,
  Chandra Shekhar Azad Park,
  Allahabad 211108 (UP.)
  Ph. 0532-2460957
  gnjhacampus@gmail.com

- Rashtriya Sanskrit Sansthan,
  Lacknow Campus
  Vishal Khan 4, Gomti Nagar,
  Lucknow: 226010 (UP.)
  Ph.: 05222393748,
  rskslucknow@yahoo.com.

- Rashtriya Sanskrit Sansthan
  K.J. Somaiya Sanskrit Vidyapeeth
  SIMSR Building, Vidya Vihar
  Mumbai 400077 (Maharashtra)
  rsksmumbai@yahoo.com

**International Research Institute of Buddhist Studies, Lucknow,** was established in 1985 as an autonomous body under the Department of Culture, Government of Uttar Pradesh. It has been and still continues to be constantly engaged in studies and research on different facets of the Buddha's life, his teachings and philosophy. The Institute has collection of books, manuscripts and many other available resources that throw light on the Buddha's philosophy, ideology, religion, art and architecture of different countries and has made them available for the researchers. Moreover, the Institute is also providing text on the Buddha in different languages, namely, Pali, Sanskrit, Tibetan etc. so that comparative studies and researches could also be done. The International Research Institute of Buddhist Studies, Lucknow also awards scholars and academicians, publishes research journals, gets books on the Buddha translated in different languages, and provides scholarships to the scholars. The Institute also organises seminars, conferences etc. and helps other institutes and organizations working on Buddha's philosophy, ideology, religion, art and architecture in organising seminars and conferences. The International Research Institute of Buddhist Studies, Lucknow has a very rich library, which is very useful for academicians and scholars working on various aspects related to the Buddha. Presently, Dr. Yogendra Singh is the Director of this Institute.

**Indian Society for Buddhist Studies (ISBS)** is an all India academic association of Buddhist Studies including its various constituents like Pali, Sanskrit, Tibetan, Chinese, Apabhramsha, Buddhist History, Art, Architecture, Archaeology, Buddhist philosophy etc. Since its very inception in December 2000, the ISBS has been dedicated to bring together the scholars of Buddhist Studies on a common academic platform. So far the Society has organised 12 annual conferences at various universities and research institutions such as:

1. Nava Nalanda Mahavihara, Nalanda, August. 2001.
2. Jammu University, Jammu, March 2003 (delayed)
3. Aligarh Sanskrit Parishad, Aligarh, March 2004 (delayed)
4. Rajasthan Sanskrit University, Jaipur (September-October, 2004)
5. Delhi University. Delhi (September 2005)
6. Panjab University, Chandigarh (September, 2006).
7. Kalidasa Sanskrit Academy, Ujjaini (October, 2007)
8. Dr. Babasaheb Ambedkar Marathwada University, Aurangabad (October, 2008)
9. Kashmir Univerist, Srinagar (September, 2009)
10. Gujarat Vidyapith, Ahmadabad (September, 2010)
11. Chintan Bhawan, Gangtok (Organized by Rashtriya Sanskrit Sansthan, New Delhi, September, 2010)
12. Doon University, Dehradun (November, 2012)

The proceedings of these conferences are published in several volumes of *The Ocean of Buddhist Wisdom.* The senior scholars are honoured with Manjushree Sammäna alongwith a citation, shawl, and Rs. 5100 in cash. It is indeed a 'Life Time Honour'. The ISBS also encourages the young scholars (upto 40 years of age) by conferring them various 'Certificates of Merit' for best papers as follows:

(i) Acharya Budhaghosa Award for Pali Literature.
(ii) Acharya Nagarjuna Award for Buddhist Sanskrit/Mahayana Philosophy
(iii) Adikari Svayambhu Award for Buddhism in Apabhrarnsha Literature

(iv) Mahapandita Rahul Sankrityayan Award for Buddhist Philosophy.

Other than Pali, Buddhism is also a part of various other languages like Sanskrit, Apabhramsha, Sinhalese, Burmese, Chinese, Thai, Tibetan, Mongolian, Korean and Japanese. Besides languages, Buddhism encompasses religion, philosophy, culture, education, history, art, archaeology, architecture etc.

It is important to understand Pali and Buddhism on account of all these branches of learning. Pali is included as one of the subjects of Civil Service Examinations of West Bengal and Bihar. This is expected to make an inroad in the job market, though in a limited manner. The Government of India has been encouraging in the development of research activities on various aspects of Buddhism, Buddhist Art, Literature and Architecture, Buddhist Tourism, and sponsoring many projects in India related to different components for further development of Pali, Tibetan, Sanskrit and other languages in particular and Buddhist Studies in general. It is being considered that Pali and Buddhist Studies are very essential for character building of students and the younger generation along with bringing peace and harmony in the society.

## NOTES

1. Winternitz Maurice/Moriz, *History of Indian Literature: Buddhist Literature and Jaina Literature*, Volume 2 (Reprint), Delhi: Motilal Banarsidass, 1993, p. 11.
2. *Ibid.*

# 8

# POTENTIALS OF BUDDHIST STUDIES WITH SPECIAL REFERENCE TO PALI LITERATURE

*Ravindra Panth*

One of the greatest scientists of our time, Albert Einstein, rightly said "Religion of the future will be a cosmic religion. It should transcend a personal God and avoid Dogmas and Theology. Covering both the naturals and the spiritual, it should be based on a religious sense, arising from the experience of all things, natural and spiritual as a meaningful unity. Buddhism answers this description. If there is any religion that could cope with the modern scientific needs, it would be Buddhism."

How true the words of Einstein are in the 21st century is a matter of great concern. Undoubtedly, the present era of scientific and technological advancement has resulted into the so called material advancement. Man seems to have achieved control over the law of nature. However, the so called scientific and technological advancement has failed to alleviate poverty that very much provides fertile ground for the growth of fundamentalism and violence. Further, the environmental degradation is yet another outcome of materialistic criteria guiding the development process under the pretext of globalisation. There is no empirical evidence to support the assumption that social and economic progress based on a materialistic conception of life can ensure happiness and well being of the humanity.

In order to bring the development process in harmony with our inner identity and character building, attention must shift to issues that help in making human a humane. It is this that makes Buddhist Studies more relevant, as it encompasses the philosophy of life completely missing in this post-modern era of developments. In the proposed panel discussion an attempt has been made not only to highlight these issues based on Pali literature, which are directly concerned with the well being of the humanity and fully capable of guiding the people to mitigate their suffering, but other potentials that the Pali literature contains.

If we ponder over the period of last sixty years, we see that it was in 1956, with the celebration of 2500 years of the Mahāparinirvāna Buddha Jayanti celebrations by the Government of India that the studies in Pali and Buddhist Studies started in India. This was the time when institutions mainly devoted to Pali and Buddhist Studies like Nava Nalanda Mahavihara (NNM), Department of Buddhist Studies, Delhi University, etc. developed. For the first time, Pali *Tipitaka* in Devanagari script along with some Commentaries (*Aṭṭhakathā*) were published by NNM. For the first time, the researchers and scholars got an opportunity to read the original words of the Buddha. Credit for all this mainly goes to three Vens Rahula Sanskrityayana, Bhadant Ananda Kaushalyayana and Bhikshu Jagadish Kashyap. Subsequently, in the following years several Deptartments of Pali and Centres of Buddhist Studies started developing throughout India, for example, in Jammu University,

Srinagar University, Central Institute of Buddhist Studies, Leh, down to Nagarjuna University in South India etc.

If we go back to the history, more than twenty-five centuries ago, Pali was the colloquial language of the part of Northern India where Gotama became the Buddha. From the time Gotama became the Buddha, until the time of his great demise (*mahāparinibbāna*), he gave thousands of sublime discourses for the benefit and happiness of many (*bahujana hitāya, bahujana sukhāya*). Within three months of the Buddha's great demise, the First Council was convened at Rajgrah, with the purpose of collecting, reciting and classifying the words of the Buddha, in order to preserve them in their pristine purity. These words are presently known as the *Tipiṭaka*. The Pali word "*piṭaka*" means "basket". "*Ti*" as a prefix in "*Tipiṭaka*" means three. Hence, *Tipiṭaka* actually means "three baskets". These are:

1. *Vinaya Piṭaka* which contains the rules of conduct pertaining to monks and nuns;
2. *Sutta Piṭaka* which contains the popular discourses given by the Buddha with apt illustrations, similes and metaphors, and;
3. *Abhidhamma Piṭaka* which contains the profound teachings of the Buddha related to the ultimate reality which elucidates the functioning and inter-relationships between mind, mental factors, material qualities, and the phenomena transcending these. It is an amalgamation of psychology and ethics in the true sense.

In addition to the *Tiiṭaka*, which contains the words of the Buddha, there are enormous number of commentaries (*Aṭṭhakathā*), sub-commentaries (*Ṭīkā*), and further sub-commentaries (*Anu-ṭīkā, Madhu-ṭīkās* etc.) which have been written by great commentators since ancient time, and are a valuable contribution to ancient Pali literature. The tradition of compiling commentaries in Pali still continues today in countries like Myanmar and Sri Lanka.

Not only does Pali literature contain the invaluable treasure of Indian civilisation, including culture, religion, and philosophy, but it also contains the great contribution of the unique message of the Buddha, which emphasises the importance of human values found in the practice of *sīla, samâdhi* and *paññā*, (morality, concentration and wisdom) that lead to the liberation of each individual, as well as provides harmony within the society, which is currently the most basic need in today's chaotic world.

The *Tipiṭaka* is an unparalleled lexicon of wisdom. It not only gives the ancient spiritual and philosophical landscape of India of more than twenty-five centuries back, but also brings back a colourful spectrum of the historical, geographical, socio-political, and cultural conditions of that time. The literature opens a window onto the administrative, educational, commercial and industrial customs of the Buddha's time. It sheds light on social conditions in the urban as well as rural life of ancient India. The India of more than 2550 years ago comes alive in this literature. It is a vast ocean overflowing with the peerless, wholesome benedictions of the Enlightened One.

The readers of this literature as well as the scholars and seekers, who wish to know the truly rich heritage of ancient India, might think that although apparently the wisdom expounded by the Buddha has disappeared from India, in reality, it flows through subsequent Indian literature. The Sanskrit literature which followed it, as well as writings in other regional languages, is full of the benevolent teachings of the Buddha. The literature of medieval saints of India is suffused with the wisdom of the Buddha. When the words of the Buddha become available in their authentic form, an analytical and comparative study of them will show that India is greatly indebted to the Buddha for his innovative thought.

The influence of the Buddha's contribution is not limited to Indian thought. The deep impact of his teaching is also visible in the spiritual thought and literature of the rest of the world. Thus, the Buddha's words carry a special significance for the human race even today. The stately grandeur of the Buddha's teachings will be verdant forever. It is the perennial forerunner of the resurrection of fallen human values. What could be more relevant to the current state of moral degradation, with its inevitable result of down-trodden people afflicted with misery?

In this way, we find that, in addition to its spiritual aspect, which is no doubt the core of ancient Pali literature, it also depicts different aspects of a society's development—paleographical, linguistic, literary, religious, philosophical, ethical, socio-political and artistic, each of which deserves patient study, special investigation, careful consideration and prudent judgment, in terms of its contribution to the society.

For this, the study of ancient Pali literature, which is undoubtedly included in Buddhist Studies, is very important and beneficial, not only for the Indians, but also for the entire human race.

# COMMENTARIES

# 9

# LIVING BUDDHISM IN ARUNACHAL PRADESH: AN ASSESSMENT

*Sristidhar Dutta*

The North-eastern states of India or the eight sisters, currently comprising of Assam, Arunachal Pradesh, Manipur, Nagaland, Meghalaya, Mizoram, Tripura and Sikkim have an important niche in the history and culture of India. Like the western frontier of India through which India was linked with western and Central Asia, the eastern frontier touching Tibet, China and South East Asia played a crucial role in shaping the history and culture of India. Since prehistoric times, there were movements of people and commodities from these two corners of the Indian subcontinent just as much as ideas percolated into the Indian heartland and beyond. The process gave rise to infinite varieties of races and cultures which give India a distinct identity.

The area is the home of a number of ethnic groups in the plains as well as on the hills with distinct socio-culture and religious identities like Saivism, Vaishnavism, Jainism, Tantrism, tribal religion, Shakti worship and Buddhism that have been prevalent here over the ages. Among the religious culture of north-east India, Buddhism has played a unique role, which is well-reflected in nicely decorated Buddhist monasteries, stupas, other Buddhist minor structures, traditional arts and crafts, rituals, festivals and dance.

It is interesting to mention that though Buddhism came to Assam from the Gangetic valley sometimes in the pre-Christian era, its impact was limited to Assam only. However, during the early medieval period, Mahayana Buddhism entered through Buddhist missionaries from Tibet to Sikkim and northern and western frontiers of present day Arunachal Pradesh. The late medieval period also witnessed the migration of numerous Buddhist tribes from Burma (Myanmar) to the border areas of Assam and Arunachal Pradesh. It is to be mentioned here that both Theravada and Mahayana Buddhist tribes are residing in various parts of north-east India. The Buddhist remains are also noticed in every nook and corner of north-east India. But unfortunately the study and research in the field of Buddhism of north-east India—its history, remains, archaeology, etc are still in its infancy.

In the state of Arunachal, we can notice both the living forms of Buddhism-Theravada form and Tibetan form of Lamaism. As many as a dozen tribes like the Monpas, the Sherdukpens, the Nahs, the Membas, the Khambas and the Khamptis. The Zhakrings and a few Chakmas follow the tenets of Buddhism. It may be mentioned here that while the Tibetan form of Buddhism, as prevalent in western and northern frontiers of the state, in considerably influenced by Lamaism; the Theravada form practiced in eastern frontier, has been following Buddhism as practiced in Myanmar and Thailand. This could have happened only due to migration of Buddhist tribes from either Tibet or Myanmar to their respective present-day settlements.

The Buddhist culture heritage of the state is evident in more than hundred Buddhist monasteries, repositories of fine arts and mural paintings, stupas, manuscripts, manuscript-paintings, colorful monastic dances and festivals, oral traditions and so on.

Thus, Buddhist heritage is an important aspect of Arunachal's culture. At the same time the impact of Buddhism in the day-to-day life of these tribes can be discerned in the state. It may be mentioned here that the Monpas and Sherdukpens believed in an old faith, which was very similar to the *bon* faith of the Tibetans. With the advent of Buddhism in the area the forces of change extended to the religious sphere. Here, Buddhism adapted to the local faith and practices of the people. Buddhist monks and monastic institutions tried to syncretically bind the two cultural traditions—this is a unique example of peaceful co-existence. Therefore, it may be pointed out that Buddhism and Buddhist monasteries have played a crucial role in transforming the life and culture of the people through interaction and exposure.[1]

The biggest monastery of Arunachal Pradesh and perhaps the second largest of Asia is the legendary 17$^{th}$ century Tawang Monastery, locally known as *Tawang Gaden Namgyal Lhatse*. It is the fountain head of the spiritual, economic and cultural life of the followers of the *Gelugpa* sect of the Mahayana school of Buddhism.[2] Thus the contribution of Lamaism practiced by Tawang Monastery in developing the socio-economic-cultural standard of the people has been quite overwhelming.

The Tawang Monastery was built not only for propagation of the Gelugpa sect of Buddhism. It served as a useful military post against the Drugpa (Bhotia) attacks.[3] Its founder, Lodre Gyatso or Mera Lama, lifted all restrictions related to military activity of the inmates of the monastery.[4] Perhaps, due to the military activities performed by the monastic authority and inmates of the Tawang Monastery the abbot of the monastery also assumed the temporal authority and he came to be known as *khenpo* or Tawang Deo.[5] The structural organization of the Government of Tawang Deo was in the form of a single great tradition of Buddhism based on elaborate administrative and cultural norms of a state-wide religion. The whole area under the Tawang Deo got divided in to three administrative centers called *dzongs,* each of which was run by two senior monks of the monastery for a term of three years and they were called *dzongpens.* They settled local disputes that were referred to them and levied *khrei* (tax) for the monastery from the peasants (*Khreipas*) from the villages under their control.

Various economic activities, such as, mural-painting, mask-making, wood-carving, local paper manufacturing, incense stick production, prayer flags idol sculpture, pottery, carpentry, carpet making are evident and are considered a by-product of the demands of religion, leading to origin and growth of various cottage industries. The social events and festivals, such as, Torgya, Losar, Choekor and pilgrimage picnics serve the dual purpose of solidarity among the members of the community and also fulfilling the socio-economic needs of the society.[6]

The tribal closeness and their socio-cultural and ethnic relations, economic linkages and dependability are attractive points that have automatically developed and have benefited the people living in the borders. Thus border-trade has been governed for ages by human groups living in border areas of neighboring countries. If similar human groups of different ethnic groups can co-exist in the international boundary, the trade relations automatically become strengthened. In the case of the North-east and specially Arunachal Pradesh some communities do live on both sides of the international borders in the eastern and north and western sections.

Data regarding the long distance trade are also suggestive of the fact that monks and monastic institutions were instrumental in augmenting long distance trade between Assam and Tibet in the Monpa region. Trade of the Monyul (Monpa region) was largely administered through the Tawang route which shaped culture and active role was played by the Tawang Monastery as well as Monpa and Sherdukpen chiefs enroute to their destinations.[9] The Singphos by the Khamptis played an equally important role in the eastern frontier in the promotion of border trade, because of their ethnic and religious similarities with the people beyond the international border. These historical examples were taken into consideration by the Government of India for successful implementation of the Look East and Act East policies.

In the eastern sector, the monasteries have been playing a very significant role in the social, educational, economic and psychological aspects of the Theravada community of Arunachal Pradesh. It acts as a binding-force, not only to unite the society but also to foster peace, non-violence and brotherhood in this region. It is still the centre of religion, culture and learning, although it has lost much of its political influence of the olden days.

Thus the monastic institutions suggest a strong organic connection with the people of the state of Arunachal Pradesh. The society provides for the logistics and provisions for the living of the monks who carry out their religious duties and the monastery in turn provides for the much-needed spiritual refuge to the common people. Thus a short of symbiotic existence is evident in the society-monastery cohabitation. This role of a social and cultural bonding has enabled the Buddhist community to be free from the turmoil in the Northeast. Not a single Buddhist youth has sought enrolment in the insurgency-dominated organizations of the North East. Further, Buddhism counters the strong influence of Christianity in the tribal areas of the North-East.

One may conclude by citing a local Buddhist intellectual: "yet must be admitted here that the process of modernization is bringing about changes both desirable and undesirable. A society in transition has put the common man into a situation where he has to fulfill the demands of an age-old tradition and at the same time respond to the changing socio-economic conditions as a result of modernization. Thus, in this light it is a matter of conjecture how the society will face the changed situation and resolve the problem."[11] The inner strength of Buddhism, it is hoped, will help the community in Arunachal Pradesh to withstand the challenges of globalization by adjusting to peaceful and non-violent methods of coexistence.

## REFERENCES

1. B.N. Jha, Buddhism, 'Buddhist monasteries and the societies of the Monyul: A Historical study', in S. Dutta & B. Tripathi (ed), *Buddhism in North-East India.* New Delhi: Indus Publishing Company, 2006. p.30.
2. Niranjan Sarkar, *Buddhism among the Monpas and Sherdukpens*, Shillong, 1980, pp. 23-36.
3. Sarkar, p. 25.
4. Sarkar.
5. B.N. Jha, p. 233.
6. Rinchen Dorjee, 'The Monpas: Their Social, economic and Religious Instructions', in S. Dutta & B. Tripathi (ed), *Buddhism in North-East India.* pp. 195-196.
7. Dorjee, p.203.
8. S. Dutta (ed), *Cross-Border trade of North-East India,* Kolkata: MAKAIAS, 2002.
9. S. Dutta and B.N. Jha, 'Historical perspectives on the cross-country trade through the Tawang Route of Arunachal Pradesh', in S. Dutta (ed) *Cross-Border trade of North-East India*, pp. 61-71
10. Dorjee, p. 203.
11. Dorjee, p. 203.

# 10

# Living Buddhism in Assam: A Vibrant Force in the Flourishing of Culture and Tradition

*Lalit Shyam*

According to different texts, in ancient times Assam was known by different names such as *Pragiyotisha* or *Pragiyotisha Pura, Kamrupa, Vaisali or Vai-sa-li-long* (Vesali of Buddhist literature) and *Moung-din-shoun-Kham* (the Land of Golden Gardens). Before partition, the boundaries of greater Assam included Arunachal Pradesh, Nagaland, Meghalaya, Mizoram, Tripura and Manipur.

Animism and shamanism, both forms of archaic tradition were prevalent in Assam in the pre-Buddhist period. It appears that before the advent of Buddhism, the indigenous people of Assam might have practiced some form of animistic religion that had a large number of adherents in the country. These could have commonalities with Brahmanical religion which came to be known as Hinduism. P.C. Choudhury states that the religious life of the people of ancient Assam was fundamentally based on pre-Aryan or non-Aryan cults and he has tried to trace the spread of Hinduism in the region. After this comes Indian culture and civilization in the form of Buddhism. Thus, the origins of Buddhism in Assam and Northeast India can be traced back to a long period. Since then, Buddhists all over Assam and Northeast India have been practicing Buddhism.

'Living Buddhism' in Assam is professed and practiced by the Tai people and certain tribes and communities and can be divided broadly into two schools, namely the southern school of Buddhism or the orthodox tradition of Buddhism, i.e. the Theravada and Northern school of Buddhism, i.e. Mahayana Buddhism.

The Buddhist population of Assam comprises of Tai tribes such as Tai Khamyang , Tai Khampti, Tai Aiton, Tai Phake, Tai Turuing, the Singphos, the Duanias, the Naga Buddhists, Burma Buddhists, Chakmas, Mogs, Mans, Nepalese, Tibetans, Bhutias, Ahom Buddhists etc.

Assam's hills and plains appear like a flat alluvial lake—land locked in the midst of hills and mountains. The land looks very dainty and picturesque, and the great peaks appear like sentinels guarding Assam's innocence and beauty. Assam has both the red river and the blue hill and therefore represents dual sceneries. The Buddhists of Assam have their own tradition, history, art, culture, language, literature sculptures, centre of learning, monasteries etc.

# INDEX